THE MUSEUM OF WITCHCRAFT

DIANE PURKISS

THE MUSEUM OF WITCHCRAFT

OBJECTS, PRACTICES, SYMBOLS:
A GUIDED TOUR TO THE OCCULT

ILLUSTRATIONS BY
BEN JONES

WELBECK

CONTENTS

INTRODUCTION

You chose to take the risk. You are in a museum, but you did not enter it as part of an organized tour group. No, you have sneaked in after dark. Perhaps it began as a prank, a bet, a bit of a lark. Some instinct deep within you told you that night was the only possible time to visit the Museum of Witchcraft. Did you hide somewhere while they locked up the building...? And are you really here of your own free will? Or has something compelled you? Dim lights in the display cases are all you have to guide your footsteps.

Every sense is tingling. Even the dust here is rich, imbued with the past. It's cold, and quiet, so why don't you feel completely alone? On your skin, you can feel the subtle caress of the power in the objects here. It makes the hairs on the back of your neck stand up. You are beginning to understand that witches have power.

Perhaps you came here in search of a particular spectacle, a particular object, a particular magic. A broomstick might be funny. A black cat might be cute. But as you make your way around, there are surprises in store. Not only the edgy moon, hurrying through the clouds, but a skull as white as she is, and then deep clefts in the earth, as well as mighty goddesses feared and loved. This is a museum of secret wisdom, knowledge lost in the past. Yet as you look and learn, you come to realize sharply that the past is not gone or dead. It is awake, and it is also seeking you to carry its power and knowledge forward into your life, your century.

Some of these truths cry out to be spoken. Now that you know, what will you do? What catches your eye? What surprises? There is a cylindrical wooden object, labelled as a dash churn. Over there, a pack of brightly painted playing cards. In a small case, a scatter of simple kitchen utensils, with handfuls of salt beside them. There is a chimney, marked with strange signs, and through the window, you can see the patterns of the stars, clear and sharp-edged, and the flight of wild birds across a cold winter sky, and with them, the slender figure of a girl – or is it an old woman?

Do you want to take flight yourself?

If you do, read on.

WAND

More a feature of fantasy fiction for children than something used traditionally by witches, the wand is another way of bringing focus to modern witchcraft practitioners, a channel for energy and feeling; the wand does nothing. It's the witch who does the magic. In modern magic, the wand is used mostly to replace the traditional knife – in circle casting, for example – and this is an obvious response to popular culture, and also to the commercialization of magic. By all means buy an expensive wand if you want to, but as with everything in witchcraft, it's better to make your own, and to make it out of something that you care about, and to spend time with it so that it's *your* wand, infused with you.

If you do choose to make one, a wand should be the same length as your arm from your elbow to the tip of your longest finger. Tradition also says that a wand should never be made from wood cut from a tree for that purpose, but should instead be made from a fallen branch or twig. In some rural kinds of witchcraft, it's customary to thank the tree in any case for its gift. Elder, rowan and hazelwood have particularly strong magical associations; the first two are protective, and the third is associated with magical knowledge through the legend of Finn McCool. There's no need for carving or augmentation, and neither is part of traditional witchcraft; symbolically, witchcraft tends to be plain, and high magic fancy. In fact, there's nothing wrong with using just a folded-up umbrella. Cleanse first, however, using a crystal or just salt.

By contrast, some African-American traditions use the staff of high magic. In Obeah, traditional West African practices have been altered by cultural hybridization; there are many uses of obeah sticks, but those practices are generally secret, and connected with the dead and the spirit world.

RITUAL

A ritual is a series of connected actions. Making bread is a ritual. Making tea or coffee is a ritual. Coronations and elections are rituals. A wedding is a ritual, and so is a funeral. All societies have rituals. How, then, can rituals be part of witchcraft?

First, rituals carry tradition with them. Admittedly, modern pagans have freely invented traditions, but most of Christmas and Thanksgiving are invented traditions, too. In following the Wheel of the Year, for example, a modern pagan may experience a sense of connectedness, including connectedness with the past. Secondly, rituals create structure. Everybody needs structure in their lives in order that there can be meaning. For example, the practice of meditation involves what is called invariance, sitting in the same place and at the same time, and removing distractions from the environment that may create too much variation.

What sits less well with witches is that rituals have rules, and the rules have to be kept. But if we make our own rules, and keep to them, that may be different. Another critical part of ritual is the use of sacred symbolism, covered elsewhere here. Anything can be sacred if we bless it with our attention, but there is a particular pleasure in the recognition that our attention joins with the attention and practices of others. We may want to reserve objects and places for specific actions. We know that if seeing is believing, doing is believing.

The other reason for rituals is their use – rituals mark rites of passage. Our Western society has no ritual for the advent of bodily maturity, or the start of menstruation, although rituals are developing around coming out as LGBT. One role of modern witchcraft might be to create ways of acknowledging important changes that are brushed under the rug in our culture. The standard structure of ritual involves separation, then a marker of change, and then reintegration. Another kind of structure might be a ritual that seeks to purify or cleanse, and perhaps above all to help us to cope with complex feelings. For some, witches may be better than Christian Western culture at acknowledging the presence of the dead, and at coping with mourning and loss.

CAULDRON

"Double, double, toil and trouble;/ Fire burn and cauldron bubble." So say the Weird Sisters in Shakespeare's play *Macbeth*. Their cauldron, the charmed pot, is full of disgusting bits and pieces, such as the finger of a baby strangled at birth. Usually depicted as black, the cauldron has become associated with grisly body parts. In fact, however, the cauldron was just a very normal way of cooking dinner in an age when few people had ovens. Suspended over a fire, it could hold a number of smaller vessels so that a meal could be cooked.

Even in *Macbeth*, what the witches do sounds strikingly like cooking. "Cool it with a baboon's blood,/ Then the charm is firm and good" sounds like something that might be said on *The Great British Bake Off*, if lemon juice were used instead of baboon blood. The cauldron is therefore another example of the way witchcraft ties into women's usual work. In using a cauldron for magic, a modern witch might simply take her favourite saucepan. Heat and cooking transform, and therefore act as triggers for other changes. When we bake, when we make dinner for friends, we are performing an ancient magic of union as powerful as the magics that protect the household from invasion. *Macbeth* wants to demonize such magic, but witches know that transitions and changes are a necessary part of life. If we celebrate some of those changes and transitions with food, we are tying the household in to the great cycles of nature itself, the wheel of birth and death.

PISCES

More water. Perhaps the most obvious of the water signs, the one that can live only in water, the one without a protective hard outer shell. And it's a mutable sign, as well as a water sign; like Aquarius, it's suspended between winter and spring... Now ruled by Neptune, it was in ancient times ruled by Jupiter, the planet of great good fortune. Like the other water signs, Pisces has often been framed as weak, prone to addiction and emotionally needy. Really? Or another example of patriarchal astrology? Just look at these famous Pisceans: Anne Bonny, pirate; Anaïs Nin; and that notorious pushover Ruth Bader Ginsburg. Pisceans are alert not only to emotions but also to aesthetics. Many great artists have planets in Pisces.

Perhaps it's the association with death that makes people uncomfortable. Pisces marks the end of the astrological year; there is death. Pisces is the old woman, the hag of the zodiac, freighted with wisdom, as opposed to boisterous baby Aries. The end also brings rebirth. The hag knows this, and can communicate her knowledge. She might choose to do this through her creative work.

Pisces is another of the signs with two faces, like Gemini and Libra; Pisces is two fish, swimming in opposite directions. Also, Pisces is a mermaid, a siren, singing of the beauty of the deep, and shape-shifting as she does. A negative astrologer might well portray Pisces as too sensitive and vulnerable for her own good, or as incapable of setting appropriate boundaries. However, such portrayals are misunderstandings of the complex, protean quality of Pisces.

She resonates with anything watery: her colour is sea green and her flower the water lily, while her tree is the willow and her gemstone is the moonstone. She understands that creativity is often a matter of patiently waiting for flow, in apparent stillness.

The Age of Pisces in astrology, lasting for 2,000 years or so, is now coming to an end. It was dominated by organized religion. The new age, of Aquarius, may be more hospitable to witches, but we also need to remember and to use everything that we were.

CANCER

Cancer is usually named as the most witchy of all the sun signs, perhaps because she is ruled by the moon, and perhaps because she is a water sign, and perhaps because Cancer rules motherhood – and all witches, regardless of gender, are mothers. Like her sister water sign, Scorpio, Cancer is often described as frighteningly possessive, clinging on with her claws, and frighteningly emotional. In the period when astrology was a male-dominated discipline, Cancer was often described as a kind of weak or wimpy sign because for Cancerians, feelings come first. It's worth reframing this as an asset, a near-magical power of discernment – Cancerians are hyper-aware of the feelings of others, which is why they make loving and caring friends, partners and parents. Just look at these famous Cancerians: Frida Kahlo; Diana, Princess of Wales; and Malala. Weak? Wimpy? I think not. Cancer helps us hold fast; Cancer is tenacious, and even in the most ferocious storm, she will not let go.

They are drawn to the sea, to the past, and to the home. Her gem is the work of the sea, the pearl, a tiny irritant turned into shining beauty. Her metal is silver. She is linked with seas and oceans, but also with breasts and breastmilk. Her tree is the sap-giving maple, and her flowers are as white as the moon – Queen Anne's lace, lily and white rose. Among animals, she rules shellfish. Her colours are blue, silver and smoke grey.

If Aquarius looks towards the future, Cancer holds the past and enables us to work with it and understand it better, more sympathetically, more kindly. Cancer is tender, thoughtful, sensitive and impressionable. Witches might want to resist the usual effort to call out faults when speaking of sun signs; not because everyone is perfect, but because the lists of thoughts are often governed by bigotry and prejudice, and this is particularly true in the case of signs identified in the past as feminine, such as Cancer. Let's embrace and honour our feelings when we think of her.

AQUARIUS

Like everything else, witchcraft is subject to change. While many witches want to emphasize tradition and history, even our ideas of what those things are tend to be relentlessly updated, and the fresh witches of TikTok offer an unprecedented recreation – witchcraft without even a trace of patriarchy's favourite fantasy, Satan. It's this new and still protean kind of witchcraft that Aquarius symbolizes. Remember the old song from the musical *Hair* which specifies that the Age of Aquarius will begin when the moon is in the Seventh House bringing about an age of peace and love? OK, the moon is in the Seventh House for two hours every day... but the idea is great. The Age of Aquarius is the new astrological age, the next 2,000 years as we move away from Piscean Christianity. Aquarius is associated with electricity, computers, democracy, freedom, humanitarianism, idealism, modernization, rebellion, nonconformity, philanthropy and humanity.

The ruler of Aquarius is Uranus, known in astrology as the Great Awakener, and the sun moves into Aquarius as the northern hemisphere begins to feel traces of warmth and light again. Imbolc (February 2) is the harbinger of spring, the time when the goddess is celebrated in her Maiden aspect; this is the goddess Brigit, who is linked to fire, smithing and poetry. She is associated with the province of Leinster, and may be linked to Brigantia, the British goddess; she also becomes the Christian St Brigid, in one of the least contentious cases of Christian appropriation of what was once a pagan figure. There is something Aquarian about the ease of this transition to the future. Brigid stays herself, flies under the radar and keeps her identity. Aquarius is cyborg, not goddess. She is made of thought, mind, word; sometimes, these can seem the very opposite of witchcraft, but witches know better. Her tree is the pear tree and her flowers are orchid and apple blossom. Her colours are blue and turquoise, and her birds are those that fly great distances. Just look at these famous Aquarians: Yoko Ono, Rosa Parks and Megan Thee Stallion. Individuality! And the power that goes with it.

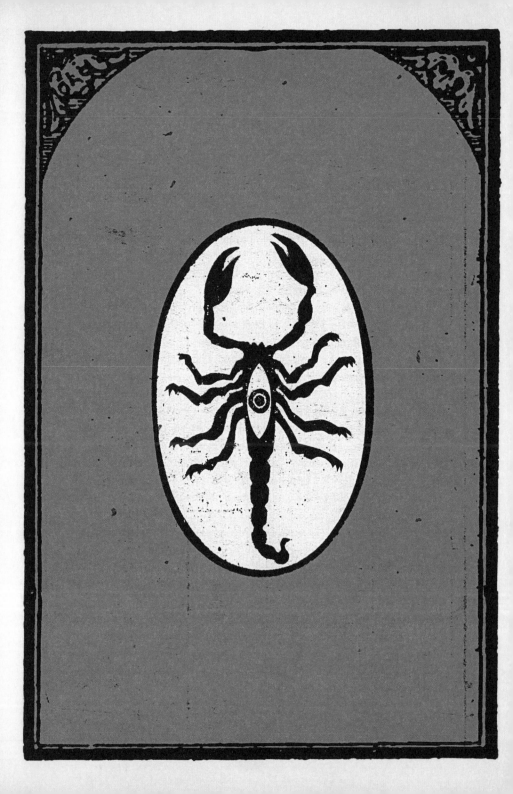

SCORPIO

This sign is associated with secret magic – aka the occult. The word literally means *hidden*.

What is it that people find scary about witches? Possessiveness. And particularly, the ability to take possession of something that properly belongs to somebody else. Scorpio incarnates that fear. But part of acknowledging the identity of the witch is to take back identities that inspire terror, saying: "Yeah. So?"

Scorpio is intense, passionate, possessive, jealous, charismatic, emotional and sexual – this sign rules the sexual organs. Good. The sign's ruling planet is Pluto, the lord of death and darkness, but in the ancient world it was Mars, the greater maleficent. The scary darkness around Scorpio is part of the scary darkness around all witches. But what's wrong with wanting to take possession of things that have been kept from us, secret knowledges and powers that belong as much to us as to anybody else? Just look at the famous Scorpio women, Marie Curie, Sylvia Plath, Hedy Lamarr, Anna Wintour. Do you feel a slight frisson of fear? Power, the ability to walk in dark places, intellectual brilliance? Why should we not have those things? Whatever your natal chart says, everybody needs to access their inner Scorpio because it's a way of acknowledging inner power.

Her gemstone is the mysterious opal with its inner fire, and she connects with all velvety dark red flowers, and with hawthorns with all their magical fairy energy. Fiery desert landscapes and countries belong to her, and so do the plants with thorns growing therein; also strong-tasting foods; and the steel or iron of the sword. Her colour is dark red. Yes, it all sounds a bit overwhelming, but that's power for you. Traditionally, Scorpios can be identified by their eyes and their direct gaze – the kind of gaze that was in the past identified with the evil eye because of its intensity. Here we are stumbling over gender norms, and the idea that women should go about with lowered eyes. Don't. Experience your power and enjoy it.

FAIRY QUEEN

The fairies are a matriarchy, ruled by a queen. She can, as the witch Isobel Gowdie said, be old and young when she pleases, and she can also be both beautiful and ugly. In stories, she is usually predatory in relation to human beings, from whom she tends to want two things: babies, or help with childbirth or breastfeeding on the one hand; and on the other, the sexual service of young men. In folklore, she is not "good" as she tends to be in popular culture, but she is immensely powerful and deeply magical, leading a kingdom of fairies which appears to comprise beings who have always been fairies, and some beings who were once human but who have been seduced or captured and are now part of the fairy realm.

In medieval literature, the fairy queen is often conflated with Persephone, queen of the underworld. King James VI of Scotland's *Daemonologie* conflates her with the goddess Diana (see page 206), but these are learned attempts to classify popular belief and assimilate it to elite culture. The same is true of the identification of Elizabeth I as the Faerie Queene, a double-edged way of describing a powerful and controversial woman ruler.

She often strikes bargains, being willing to exchange magical healing powers for babies, and prophetic capacities for male sexual services. She is described in a series of Scottish ballads, all of which centre on a male figure whose name is something like Thomas, a figure who is both her captive and her lover. These tales, widely told in Aberdeenshire, match the confession of the accused witch Andrew Man, who describes a sexual relationship with the queen of the fairies, and a number of children with her. Man is a healer and a seer, deriving his powers from the queen.

I BID THE MOUNTAINS SHAKE, THE EARTH TO RUMBLE
AND THE GHOSTS TO COME FORTH FROM THEIR
TOMBS. THEE ALSO, LUNA, DO I DRAW FROM THE SKY,
THOUGH THE CLANGING BRONZE OF TEMESA STRIVE
TO AID THY THROES; EVEN THE CHARIOT OF THE SUN,
MY GRANDSIRE, PALES AT MY SONG.

AND THE CLEAR MOON, BESET BY DREAD
INCANTATIONS, GREW DIM AND BURNED WITH A DARK
AND EARTHY LIGHT, JUST AS IF THE EARTH CUT HER
OFF FROM HER BROTHER'S REFLECTION AND THRUST
ITS SHADOW ATHWART THE FIRES OF HEAVEN.
LOWERED BY MAGIC, SHE SUFFERS ALL THAT PAIN,
UNTIL FROM CLOSE QUARTERS SHE DROPS FOAM
UPON THE PLANTS BELOW.

MOONFOAM

The aim of drawing down the moon is to collect the lunar power that accumulates from the proximity of the moon to the earth, whether in the form of plants with extra potency from the moon's rays or in a concentrated form as "moonfoam", *aphroselenon*.

This may possibly be *Ipomoea alba*, or moonflower, which is a member of the *Ipomoea* genus along with morning glory and is recognized as having hallucinogenic seeds and being mildly toxic. The flowers open quickly in the evening and last through the night, remaining open until touched by the morning dew.

As Sextus Julius Africanus, an historian who died in the early third century CE, tells us in his collection of interesting facts entitled *Kestoi*, this moonfoam is gathered from the dew of plants and the rays of moonbeams, and Roman poet Lucan and other sources refer to the foam of the moon that appears when the moon is drawn down by magic, as in the charm opposite.

Zosimus of Panopolis, an alchemist from the third century CE, links *aphroselenon* with the rays of the moon, since at the waning (or drawing down?) of the moon there is an outflow of light that bears the particular lunar nature. This magical substance might be used for various magical ends, but Lucan depicts the witch Erictho using the moonfoam in her gruesome reanimation of a corpse for necromancy (see page 152):

> Then she began by piercing the breast of the corpse with fresh wounds, which she filled with hot blood; she washed the inward parts clean of clotted gore; she poured in lavishly the poison that the moon supplies.

It has been suggested by some that moonfoam is exuded by the moon at the moment of orgasm, just as mandrakes are formed under the gallows by the ejaculate of the dying man (see Mandrake, page 42). These bodily fluids, like pieces of the dead (see Necromancy), are traces of continuing vitality that can be used magically as a source of energy. The witch Medea proclaims:

> Summaries like this one stress the fearsome power of the moon and the moonfoam, but they also can't help but note just how strong a substance it really is.

TOADS, FLIES, WEASELS, FROGS

English witches were believed to keep familiars, demons that took the form of small animals. These were shape-shifters, capable of entering the houses of other people under the door, down the chimney, or through a crack in the window, and so could be understood as an extension of the witch's own body, a part of her that could be sent beyond her physical form. Finally, they could be understood as the witch herself, transformed into an animal.

Most people know about witches and cats (see page 146). However, the historical record shows a much wider range of familiar animals. Flies, spiders, dogs, weasels, ferrets, bees, moles, rats, mice and snails. Yes, demon snails. These animals would offer the witch their help and ask for food. Sometimes, familiars were passed down from one witch to another. While they make their first appearance in an English trial in the Chelmsford case of 1566, an ecclesiastical case from 1530 draws a link between a toad and a witch. Is there something particular about toads? Ambivalent creatures, they were believed to have a jewel in their heads but were also known to be poisonous.

It has been argued by the historian Emma Wilby, among others, that the familiar was really a fairy, likely to be the household brownie, covered in fur. This certainly echoes the trials, which indicate that the familiar was rewarded with a bowl of cream – a traditional gift for a household spirit helper – but the connection with familiars who take the form of hairless or very small animals is less plausible. However, it is certainly right to say that witch-hunters such as Matthew Hopkins turned the familiar into a weapon against the witch, an elusive piece of unarguable evidence, who may at one time simply have been the pet of an elderly woman. This is supported by the story of William Harvey, the scientist who took it upon himself to dissect a toad kept by an elderly woman accused of witchcraft. His goal was to prove her innocence, and also to show her that she had no magical powers. The woman was furious with Harvey, and attacked him for killing her pet.

WITCH MARKS ON BUILDINGS

There are hundreds of them, perhaps thousands – when Historic England asked the public to help by photographing and identifying witch marks, they received over 600 responses. Apotropaic witch marks survive on many buildings, and also on some natural landscapes. (*Apotropaic* literally means to turn away, so the effect of the mark is to repel.) There are several different kinds, but most repeat the idea of the pentacle, an endless knot or line, and therefore a perfect container without a point of entry. Sympathetic magic means that placing such a mark transfers the same perfect enclosure to the building on which it is placed.

One recognizable example is the hexafoil, or daisy wheel, which is a six-petalled daisy enclosed in a circle – a continuous line, enclosed in another continuous line. Obviously, this can connect with other circular symbols, ranging from the Sun to the Wheel of the Year, but it seems more likely that all of these were interpreted in the same way, as endless, as powerful and as impermeable. The six-pointed star, or the letters V and M intertwined, is sometimes read as the Virgin Mary but is perhaps just another set of intersecting infinite lines.

Most of them survive in buildings dating from the medieval period through to the early nineteenth century, so that they predate and also post-date the period of the witch trials, illustrating the extraordinary continuity of ritual practice despite ecclesiastical condemnation. They also traverse the entire class spectrum, surviving in manor houses and cottages, pubs and smithies. A room at the country house Knole in Kent, built to accommodate James VI of Scotland and I of England after the Gunpowder Plot, contains many witch marks, including crosshatched marks. King and commoner were alike in their wish to find a safe and fully enclosed space. Elsewhere, marks might be used as an effort to seal what were seen as problematic openings in the ground (see Cleft in the Earth, page 100) which might emit dangerous supernatural beings. We all want to shut ourselves away sometimes.

WITCH MARKS ON THE BODY

In England, the witch mark was some kind of bulge or swelling on the body which was supposed to act as a nipple, allowing a demon familiar to feed on the blood of the witch. The first reference to witch marks in England comes from the Chelmsford trial of 1566.

Separately, the idea widespread on the Continent and in Scotland was that the devil left a mark on all his devotees, typically on the right hand or the forehead, and this was sometimes called *the devil's spot*, or *punctum*. It might be shaped like the footprint of an animal, or like an astrological sign, but it could be detected because it was impervious to pain, like a piece of dead flesh. Surgeons would shave the entire body in their search for such a mark. Judges and juries uncomfortable with convictions based on the witch's confession alone liked this "scientific" evidence.

In England, the search for the teat was usually conducted by midwives, contradicting the idea that midwives were more likely to be accused; they were more likely to work with accusers to discover material evidence. Some comic and sad misreadings of bodily parts ensued, since one group of midwives identified what was very clearly the clitoris as a witch mark, while another group thought that haemorrhoids might act as suckling teats.

The whole notion seems to come from an urgent wish for the body of the witch to be recognizable, and also different from the bodies of others. And yet this became connected with grotesque misreadings of normal female anatomy. The English witch mark, the teat, was usually sought and found on the lower body of the witch, because female genitalia were diabolical in any case, the mouth of hell, and the clitoris, whose existence was denied by most anatomists, was seen as especially peculiar. And yet the teat was more a parody of motherhood than of sexuality: the witch as bad mother nourished demons on blood instead of milk.

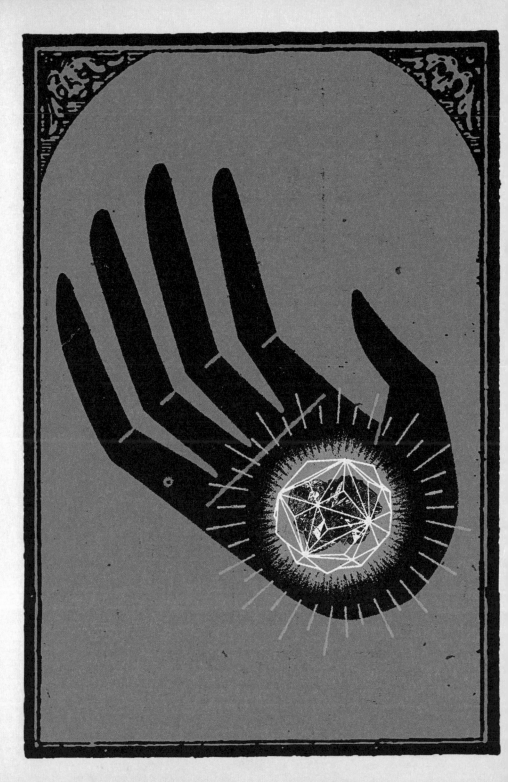

CLEAR CRYSTAL

Scrying is the act of gazing into a reflective or translucent object such as glass, water, a mirror or a crystal to see otherwise, a way of working around time and the obvious. In the past, very many kinds of objects had been used. Clear crystals are currently used by modern pagans – to enhance mental energy or for magical wishes – but these are not a traditional part of Western witchcraft. The only role of a clear crystal in traditional Western witchcraft is as a scrying device, and even then other devices were often preferred, such as the Aztec mirror used by John Dee, advisor to Elizabeth I. The whole idea of crystals is for the most part historically fairly recent, dating back only to the nineteenth century. When witches in earlier periods sought out second sight, they more commonly used the riddle and shears, a circular sieve with a pair of shears balanced in it. As the sieve was turned, the shears moved, pointing in a particular direction, and enabling the witch to discern lost items, perpetrators of magical harm, or buried treasure. By contrast, Scottish claims to second sight typically used no equipment at all. The Brahan Seer, also known as Coinneach Odhar (Dark Kenneth), is thought to have used an adder stone, a stone with a hole in the middle, to see his visions; his birth and death dates are disputed, but there are two records for a Coinneach Odhar accused of witchcraft.

The underlying idea behind modern uses of clear crystals is sympathetic magic. Because the crystal is transparent and focuses light, it is assumed that it will enable a fresh and focused way of seeing, and because it is transparent, it appears to offer the power to see through. However, and interestingly, the traditional crystal ball has been all but abandoned on the grounds that it is now associated with popular culture and with fraudulence. There is perhaps an element of racism in this thinking: crystal balls were associated particularly with Romani ("gypsy") people.

IRISH GODDESSES

There is no pantheon of deities in Celtic mythology, and the idea of gods may be alien to Celtic thinking. Yet when modern pagans first began to speak about the goddess, they often meant a particularly British conception of her. To be sure, the idea of the goddess is intrinsically syncretic (a synthesis of various cultures), and Diana and Hekate have also played an important role in thinking about what female power might be like, but the idea that a triple goddess who exemplifies the female life cycle might have a connection to witchcraft has been stubborn and persistent, in part because goddesses of this kind do appear in the surviving literature of the peoples of north-western Europe. Caveats are vital: we have no material whatsoever from the pagan past which hasn't been transcribed and probably revised by Christians, who often reshaped older beliefs in order to make an Other for themselves.

With that in mind, the goddesses of insular northern Europe are a compelling and seductive group if we are looking for female power. They are warriors and queens and they offer an unapologetic image of female mastery – and if it's a fantasy, it's a fairly old fantasy, dating back at least to the Celtic revival, and if it's mostly a male fantasy, why not take the image back from them?

Ceridwen (see page 134) is perhaps the goddess with the most obvious witchy connotations, given her magic cauldron (see page 14), although the Greek witch Medea also had a cauldron and used it in the same way, for regeneration and rebirth. A shape-shifter, with a hideously ugly son and a beautiful daughter, she is also the mother of the prophet Taliesin, and is linked with the figure of the hag, the Cailleach (pronounced Kolyuk), and particularly the sovereignty hag of Ireland.

Like the fairy, the hag can be old or young, beautiful or ugly as she likes, and the name is also given to the last sheaf of a harvest, itself often ritualistically treated by being dressed as a woman and given an apron full of bread, cheese and a sickle.

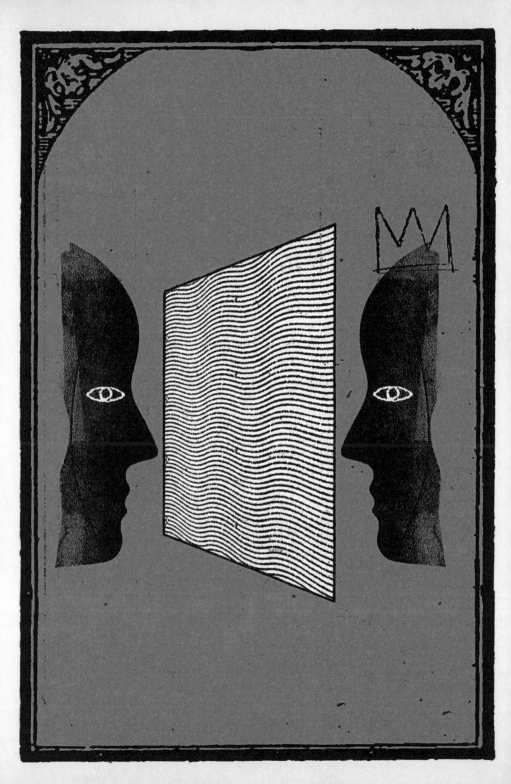

MAGICK

Both a noun and a verb, *magic* is what witches do. But how can we explain exactly what they do? In the *Oxford English Dictionary*, magic is defined by a series of negatives: it is supernatural, but it falls outside religion; it is about change, but it falls outside science – except, of course, when it doesn't, given that astrology leads directly to astronomy, and alchemy to chemistry. However, magic might also be defined as areas of religion and science that are not yet rationally understood. In that sense, witches might recognize something in quantum physics, say, as belonging to a world of transformation or even just an idea of matter in constant motion which is inimical to ideas of reality in the everyday. Witches might recognize in the amorousness of matter – more usually known as gravity – something they have long understood.

All magic is shadowed not only by Christian reframing as Satanism, but by the figure of the stage magician; the *Oxford English Dictionary* insists on bringing conjurers and fake magicians into consideration, along with magicians who have real powers though wholly derived from the devil. Both Satanism and conjuration are ways of saying that the magic of witches does not exist. Reginald Scot wrote in the sixteenth century that witches could not possibly do magic because they were just elderly women living in villages; others, such as James VI of Scotland, suggested that the heavy lifting was being done by male forces (namely, devils).

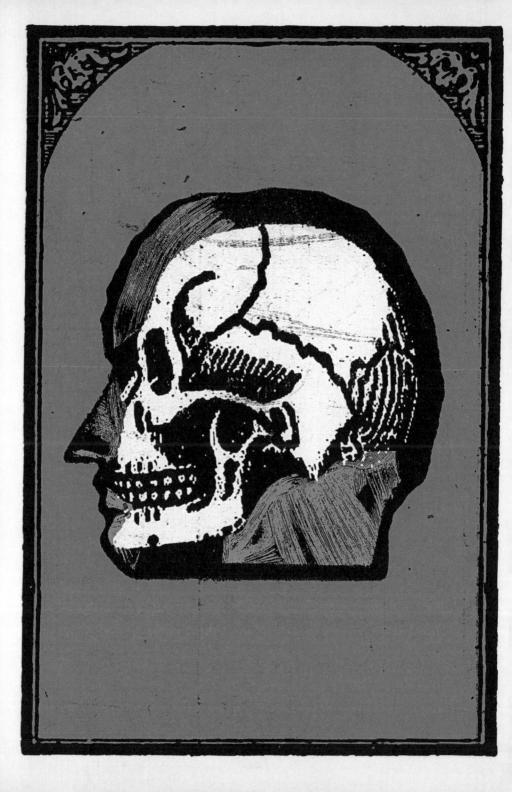

SKULL AND FLESH

Whatever is dark and scary is the domain of the witch. In history, witches have always managed the liminal, and the fears that go with it. It therefore follows that part of magic is the ability to deal with death and with the bodies of the dead. To be sure, the witches in Shakespeare's *Macbeth* are caricatures, as are those in Lucan's Roman epic, *Pharsalia*, but all of them use bodies to work their magic. What lies behind this idea? Is it just a libel?

When somebody dies suddenly, unexpectedly or young, there is an assumed reservoir of psychic energy unused by that person which can be deployed by somebody else through contact with that person and their body. This doesn't have to be either grotesque or irreverent. Of course, it was portrayed as negatively as possible by mainstream culture, but it may actually be true that one definition of a witch is someone who has an unusual relationship with the dead in general and dead bodies in particular. That unusual relationship might be characterized by a lack of disgust, by a willingness to see the dead as still having needs – the need to be remembered, the need to be mourned, the need to be connected with the living – but with that awareness might well come a healthy fear. Not very long ago, most people believed that the recently deceased would try to get back their lives, families and property if they could, and that those who died in battle, by suicide or in childbirth were especially likely to make the attempt. In the past, one of the important roles played by witches was managing the restless dead – containing them, to some extent controlling them. These dead remained restless until all the flesh had rotted from their bones. Once reduced to a bare skull, they became so safe that even depressed intellectuals like Hamlet are comfortable philosophizing over them.

MANDRAKE

A mandrake is the root of a plant, of the genus *Mandragora* found in the Mediterranean region, or from other species, such as *Bryonia alba*, the English mandrake. In the past, mandrake was often made into amulets that were believed to bring good fortune, for example, or cure sterility. In one superstition, people who pull up this root will be condemned to hell, and the mandrake root screams and cries as it is pulled from the ground, killing anyone who hears it.

It has been suggested that it was an ingredient in witches' flying ointment, but that in itself is mostly a fantasy of the people who wanted to execute witches, rather than something we learn from the witches themselves. The suggestion comes from the idea that night flying is the result of hallucinogenic drugs, an idea that is frequently suggested and sometimes supported by archaeological work, though there is little real evidence in its favour, and which also owes something to the tendency to pathologize frequently reported experiences. However, mandrake could also be a sedative, as Shakespeare understood: "Not poppy, nor mandragora,/ Nor all the drowsy syrups of the world,/ Shall ever medicine thee to that sweet sleep/ Which thou owedst yesterday."

Witches digging mandrake roots at night at the foot of a gallows are shown in a painting from about 1650 by David Teniers the Younger (1610–90). Scavenging items connected with violent death is commonplace in depictions of witches, but in this case, it connects with the idea that mandrake is created when a man being hanged involuntarily ejaculates, and his semen falls to the ground. Semen was believed to contain tiny homunculi that could embed themselves in the womb, so why not also the ground?

In Norse mythology, mandrake was especially associated with the god Odin, who hung on the ash tree for nine days to gain wisdom; the mandrake was said to spring from his semen. Poet John Donne wrote, "Get with child a mandrake root"; he was describing something that was supposed to be impossible, and therefore magical.

A SAVAGE PLACE! AS HOLY AND ENCHANTED
AS E'ER BENEATH A WANING MOON WAS HAUNTED
BY WOMAN WAILING FOR HER DEMON–LOVER!

WANING MOON

Are these the witchiest lines in all of literature (Coleridge's *Kubla Khan*)? We are deep in a chasm in the ground, and we stand beneath a waning moon as the ghost of a woman, deserted by her demon lover, wails aloud. The waning moon is a time when energy and power withdraw, like the ebbing tide, so it is also a time of loss and mourning. Yet when the moon begins to wane, that might mean a witch elsewhere is drawing it down, pulling on the thread, and making it lessen. The ghostly woman in the poem may be wailing a magical spell to pull her lover (see Thessalian Wheel, page 162).

But if the lunar tide is withdrawing from some, it may be because others are using its magic. As we watch the moon wane, we see power. Most astrologers now will frame the waning moon as an opportunity to calm down, slow down and take stock, but historians of witchcraft might prefer to emphasize the potential ability to control and manage the moon exactly when she is weak. Actors do not always work in the direction that nature works, but sometimes work against it, as the witch in Lucan's ancient Roman epic *Pharsalia* does, using her magic to double the darkness of the night so that scavengers flee the battlefield. It is under the waning moon that this witch is able to reanimate the dead. In other words, the waning moon is the time of necromancy (see page 152) and also of the revival of what has been lost or forgotten, suppressed or buried.

The witch begins her incantation with a noise that is not even animal in its terrible power. It is a sound that contains the barking of dogs, the howling of walls, the cries of the owl and the thunder of waves crashing on rocks – all the powers of nature at her most terrifying. Before we decide that this is not what witches do, and that all such descriptions are a calumny, let's consider the enormous amount of power implied.

ERCE, ERCE, ERCE, EARTH'S MOTHER,
MAY THE ALL-RULER GRANT YOU,
THE ETERNAL LORD,
FIELDS GROWING AND FLOURISHING,
PROPAGATING AND STRENGTHENING,
TALL SHAFTS, BRIGHT CROPS,
AND BROAD BARLEY CROPS,
AND WHITE WHEAT CROPS,
AND ALL EARTH'S CROPS.

MAY THE ETERNAL LORD GRANT HIM, AND HIS HOLY
ONES, WHO ARE IN HEAVEN, THAT HIS PRODUCE BE
GUARDED AGAINST ANY ENEMIES WHATSOEVER, AND
THAT IT BE SAFE AGAINST ANY HARM AT ALL, FROM
POISONS/WITCHCRAFTS SOWN AROUND THE LAND.
NOW I BID THE RULER, WHO SHAPED THIS WORLD,
THAT THERE BE NO SPEAKING-WOMAN NOR ARTFUL
MAN THAT CAN OVERTURN THESE WORDS THUS SPOKEN.

AN ANGLO-SAXON CHARM FOR
FIELD GROWTH

The whole charm cleanses a field that has been failing. It comes from the eleventh century, but parts of it are clearly pre-Christian, though it survives in a clerical and Christian text. Its pagan origins show in the reference to the land as the mother of men, and its insistence that the land be a fertile mother to those who depend on her. But it's also a charm for a world of terrifying powers who oppose human needs.

And with it, we dive into the mucky world of witchcraft survival. The following single verse has only a tenuous relationship with the rest of the charm, which is about ploughing and sowing, but somebody thought it was important enough to include. What we can know is dependent on such tiny anonymous choices; scribes who choose to stop transcribing what witches say because they already have enough evidence for conviction, or Christian scribes who decide it can't hurt to include the words in front of them. We will never know why.

Notice the reference to magic practitioners in the penultimate line. To do magic is also to defeat the magic of others. Also, nobody really knows the meaning of *Erce*. Some people think she is a forgotten earth goddess, and others think that the word is just an invocation, a cry. Tacitus in his *Germania* says: "the English...were goddess-worshippers; they looked on the earth as their mother."

If you like this, try the Nine Herbs Charm from the same period.

BUT TRUE LOVE IS A DURABLE FIRE
IN THE MIND EVER BURNING
NEVER SICK, NEVER OLD, NEVER DEAD
FROM ITSELF NEVER TURNING.

HEARTH

The hearth has its own goddess, and in the ancient world, she was called Hestia, or Vesta; the latter name gives us the Vestal Virgins, keepers of the flame who had to remain virginal to serve it. Provided they remained chaste, the Vestal Virgins had immense and unique powers, long before Christianity created convents. They retired around the age of 40, and after that were free to marry.

The choosing ceremony was known as a *captio* (capture). Once a girl was chosen to be a Vestal, the pontifex pointed to her and led her away from her parents with the words, "I take you, amata [beloved], to be a Vestal priestess, who will carry out sacred rites which it is the law for a Vestal priestess to perform on behalf of the Roman people." So long as their bodies remained unpenetrated, the walls of Rome would, it was believed, remain intact. Their flesh belonged to Rome, and when they died, whatever the cause of their death, their bodies remained within the city's boundary. Spontaneous extinction of the sacred flame for no apparent reason might be understood as a prodigy, a warning that the *pax deorum* (peace of the gods) was disrupted by some undetected impropriety, unnatural phenomenon or religious offence.

In other words, the hearth of Vesta *was* Rome. Many of these ideas were simply transferred to the domestic fireplace, without much emendation for a Christian culture. The individual hearth within the house represented that household. The chimney (see page 198) could be an aperture where dark forces might enter the house, and the best way of preventing that was to tend the hearth, to "keep the home fires burning", maintaining a protective magic through the knowledge of fire.

Sweeping the hearth clear of ash involved an understanding of fire. So did making a fire, using kindling gathered from woodlands to set on fire the larger logs that might burn all night. There's a magic quality to the hearth which protects those who need the warmth of the fire from its ferocity, and many old domestic hearths bear witch marks (see page 30).

But any physical fire will eventually sputter and die. Not so the fire of love (see opposite page).

FLIGHT

An iconic part of the image of the witch, the broomstick is meant to be the mechanism by which she flies through the air, like a balloon or a glider. However, witches could fly long before they were associated with brooms. Folklore mentions witches flying with pitchforks, staffs, plant stands, hurdles, bowls and pig troughs. The classical world gave us flying witches, in the form of the Roman birdlike witch, the striga. The *Errores Gazarorum*, from 1437, asserted that demons presented a stick with flying ointment to all new witches, while everyone agreed that church bells could endanger the flight of witches, and one confession from a witch claimed that the ringing of the bells actually brought her down from the sky. Johannes Nider's *Formicarius* (1436–38) recorded the case of a woman who rubbed salve on her body while saying a charm, and then fell into a deep sleep – she believed she was flying but was actually dreaming. The Benandanti (good walkers) of Fruili, Italy, flew on animals to fight against evil witches to protect the fertility of the land, a point they tried to explain to inquisitors in the 1570s, while the Sicilian doñas de fuera – fairies – made contact with girls who had a sweet blood, supplied them with magical animals, and encouraged them to fly to take part in a sabbath with the fairies. Strange efforts have been made by many to explain all this as the results of hallucinations. However, it is quite usual for human beings to dream that they are flying. In rapid eye movement sleep, in which our bodies feel as if they are paralyzed, the parts of our brain responsible for waking us start to wake up, and the neighbouring brain cells that locate us also awaken, which gives us the sensation of being weightless, or of flying, and then of falling to the ground.

When culture gets involved, storytelling and interpretation begin. Because we all tend to imagine a universe with the heavens above us, the principal significance we attach to flying is mastery and power, and also the ability to see into the lives of others and of riding on the storm. Witches...

OATH

There was a time when an oath was almost a physical power. It had to be guaranteed by a supernatural being *given* the specific task of ensuring that oaths were kept.

Zeus Horkios was the upholder of oaths and promises, and Zeus Herkeios also protected the hearth. In ancient Roman religion and law, the *sacramentum* was an oath or vow that rendered the swearer *sacer* – "given to the gods", in the negative sense if he violated it. *Sacramentum* also referred to a thing that was pledged as a sacred bond, and consequently forfeit if the oath were violated. Both instances imply an underlying *sacratio*, act of consecration.

Sacramentum is the origin of the English word *sacrament*, a transition in meaning which is reflected by Apuleius, the second-century writer who used the word to refer to religious initiation.

The *sacramentum* that renders the soldier *sacer* helps explain why he was subjected to harsher penalties, such as execution and corporal punishment, that were considered inappropriate for civilian citizens, at least under the Republic. In effect, he had put his life on deposit, a condition also of the fearsome *sacramentum* sworn by gladiators. In the rare case of punishment by decimation, the surviving legionaries were often required to renew their oath, affirming the role of state religion as the foundation of Roman military discipline.

Heitstrenging is an Old Norse term referring to the swearing of a solemn oath to perform a future action. They were often performed at Yule and other large social events, where they played a role in establishing and maintaining good relationships, principally between members of the aristocratic warrior elite. The oath-swearing practice varied significantly, sometimes involving ritualized drinking or placing hands on a holy pig, which could later be sacrificed. The practice continued in an altered manner after the Christianization of Scandinavia.

Related to the concept of swearing allegiance to a ruler in return for a ring, oaths were also sworn upon rings without an exchange of ownership. In *Hávamál*, Odin describes how he broke a ring-oath (Old Norse: *baugeið*), and now cannot be trusted.

DEER

Sometimes called the fairies' cattle, deer are a delicate and half visible presence in the landscape, like the fairies themselves. Also like the fairies themselves, they are creatures of great power. In mating season, the woods ring with the sound of stags belling.

Many Otherworld stories from Celtic language cultures include tales of human beings who can be transformed into deer. This includes the wife of Finn McCool, Saba, who is a sweet and vulnerable doe when he first encounters her; recognized by his magical hounds, she becomes human when she enters his territory, but when she is persuaded to recross the threshold by her former magical master, the Dark Druid, she becomes a doe again. However, her son with Finn McCool is discovered as a child, hiding in the woods, and is at once named Oisin, Little Fawn.

In the eleventh-century tale of Culhwch and Olwen, Culhwch is helped to hunt an enchanted boar by a supernatural stag with which he can communicate, while in the first of the *Mabinogi* (compiled in the eleventh century), Pwll lets his hounds eat from a stag which is the quarry of Arawn, king of Annwn, the Welsh Otherworld; these stories position stags as keepers of the gateway between worlds, bridges from underworld and Otherworld to the human realm.

The kinship between magic and deer is retained as late as the Scottish witchcraft persecutions. Many witches confessed to seeing tutelary spirits in the form of stags or does: Andrew Man, for example, who was burnt as a witch in 1598, saw his fairy guide rising out of snow in the form of a stag.

In the mythology of the Celtic peoples, the stag is the king of the forest, and also represents the power of the midday sun. Efforts to identify a Celtic God with horns have faltered – many antlered local tribal deities have been discovered, such as Cernunnos of the Parissi, but no overarching set of beliefs can be established with certainty. Nevertheless, there is archaeological evidence of the use of stag antlers in a variety of magical rituals, and also some evidence of animal sacrifice. The centre of animal magic, deer represent the possibility of crossing the boundaries between worlds.

THE GREEN MAN

Ian Anderson of Jethro Tull sings of Jack in the Green, the power that Dylan Thomas describes as the electric energy that pushes the flower out of the green stem. Undeterred by motorways and power lines, as Anderson has noticed, Jack can still be seen in every blade of grass that grows through the pavement. In folklore, Jack is a costume worn by chimney sweeps, who dress up in all their best clothes, many of them wearing ribbons, one of them dressed as a lord and another as a lady, and one or two dressed as clowns. The Jack in the Green was a man standing inside a wooden or basketwork frame, from well above his head to his ankles, on which were fixed real leaves and flowers, as if he were a moving bush, a dancing tree. Oddly, Jack is a chimney demon, with the energy of fire – and disappeared when boys ceased to be chimney sweeps. And he was always regional, making it difficult to connect him with the so-called Green Man – but there might be an underlying connection through the experience of the seasons.

The Green Man is a very recent creation in folklore studies, and the use of the phrase to designate a foliate head dates back only to 1939. However, the whifflers of Tudor England, whose role was to drive back the crowds from a procession route, were called wild men and were covered in leaves, and men in green often featured at court entertainments. Folklorist John Aubrey mentions the Green Man as interchangeable with the Wild Man, and pub signs in the seventeenth century showed the wild man as a kind of Hercules, with a green club and green leaves about his groin and head. The leafy face is something repainted recently. However, this might be a case of folklore catching up slowly with something that people want to see and experience, the continuity of green even through its disappearance in winter. If a symbol works, it doesn't really matter if it is recent or ancient. Whether or not it's traditional, Britain is now firmly the land of the Green Man.

HERBS

As any cook will tell you, herbs are magical, and they are transformative. However, the idea that witches in medieval times were mainly known for their herbalism is a mistake: *every* woman in the past was an amateur herbalist; knowing about herbs and their healing properties was part of life for everyone. Traditions of herb use were passed down through families, and recipe books frequently contained magic spells, healing remedies and recipes all jumbled together. Herbs have always played a vital part in magic, and some magic users have discovered properties in herbs not known to conventional Western medicine.

The Delphic Oracle, a priestess through whom the god Apollo spoke, is said to have sat above a brazier on which herbs burned, generating what may have been hallucinogenic smoke. In the Caribbean today, European witchcraft has been hybridized with African beliefs to create, among other things, rootwork (see Hoodoo, page 170). Rootworkers, or swampers, learned Native American traditions as well as European ones, and turned them into the only medicine available to slaves on plantations in the Caribbean and the American antebellum South. African plants brought from Africa to North America were cultivated by enslaved African Americans for medicinal and spiritual use for the slave community. The roots of High John the Conqueror were placed in mojo bags for love, luck and protection; the herb evokes the spirit of John de Conquer, who symbolizes ties to enslaved ancestors through the "soil of the South". Frederick Douglass was said to have used a High John root for protection; Zora Neale Hurston compared the power of High John to that of King Arthur. It is probably *Ipomoea purga*, and therefore related to moonfoam (see page 26).

TAROT

Tarot cards are a deck of 78 cards, divided into major and minor Arcana. The major Arcana, or trumps, contain 22 cards of great symbolic significance, beginning with the Fool, and including the Magician, the High Priestess, Death, the Devil and the World. The minor Arcana resemble a modern deck of playing cards, divided into four suits that correspond roughly with those in a modern deck, but with each suit containing four rather than three court cards. While invented for playing a card game called *Tarocchi* in Renaissance Italy, tarot cards progressively acquired magical significance and are now mostly used for divination.

THE MAGICIAN

In some packs, he is called the Juggler or even the Jongleur. He represents the power to make things change, and particularly the strength of will that accompanies such changes. He is the forceful dynamism and energy required for any activity in life. As part of a journey towards meaning, he represents the energy and excitement of the soul as it begins its quest, and particularly the moment when we are young enough to confuse pretence with reality. In the Goddess Tarot deck, the Magician, represented by Isis, the Egyptian fertility goddess, represents the power to bring back that which has been abandoned or forgotten. When the Magician appears in a reading, he affirms the choices you have made, and tells you that you are wherever you are meant to be, and that you have the power you need to manifest your goals. You can dream, but you can also act. The Magician also represents a moment – or perhaps even a half-hour – of dazzling insight, a moment of revelation. But he also warns us to be casual, because such moments can deceive us. In front of him on the table lie a range of materials needed for magic or, in some decks, for tricking gullible people into parting with their money. Associated with the alchemists of the Renaissance, the Magician promises to turn base earth into gold, but he also warns us to keep a close watch on anyone who is as interested in gold as he is.

THE MOON

See also other articles on the moon (pages 44, 78, 88 and 112).

The moon is usually portrayed as secondary to the sun, a mere reflection, and also as a distortion of the sun. To witches, however, the moon is sovereign because it represents what goes on in the silence of our lives, what happens at night, in dreams, imagination. It represents our fears, and because of that, it can seem a card of delusion and even madness. However, it doesn't have to be like that. The moon is the mistress of remembrance, a representation of the parts of nature we try not to know about, and yet those are the same parts of nature that fascinate us.

The Moon is also the card of poetry, the magic that opens the hidden parts of the universe and makes them more vivid than the common sense of daylight. In Pamela Colman Smith's design, a wolf howls at the moon, and a hare crouches in its light. Although many guides to tarot say that the moon shows all is not as it seems is not to say it has no truth, but that the daylight world has no place for the kind of truth it offers. The beauty of the moon has been lost to readings that insist it is ominous, and witches need to take back its imaginative potency. Sylvia Plath understood its power: for her, the moon suggested a white knuckle, clenched in anxiety, that dragged the dark sea after it. The expression on the face of the moon struck her as open-mouthed despair. Emily Dickinson, on the other hand, saw the moon as a queenlike presence with the universe as her shoe and the stars a glittering belt. The moon is a shared site, but everybody sees her differently.

THE QUEENS

Every suit in tarot contains a queen. While some designers now emphasize the gender queerness of the page cards, sometimes redesignated the princesses, the queens remain symbolic of the femininity we may all share, just as the Knights and Kings represent masculinity – not the same as gender identity.

What is a queen? In looking at tarot cards, we usually think of the Queen as the consort of the King. But what if the tarot Queens are Queens Regnant, like Mary Tudor, or her sister Elizabeth Tudor, or Mary Queen of Scots? How does that change what they mean when we see them as part of ourselves?

Because the Queen card can often stand in for a mother figure, she may indicate the kinds of difficulties between mothers and daughters that can and do often scupper relationships, even between witches.

The Queen of Cups – profoundly understanding of the feelings of others, and often deeply loved and deeply lovable, capable of drawing people by the heart, including and perhaps even primarily through art (visual or verbal). ISFP (Myers-Briggs). The Queen of Cups is Cancer, the Dolphin.

The Queen of Pentacles – often dismissed as a housewife, but actually a shrewd businesswoman who understands the power of money and uses her hands to make a place in the world. ISTJ (Myers-Briggs). The Queen of Pentacles is Capricorn, the Deer.

The Queen of Swords – a brilliant intellect, as shining as a sword, and aware of the darkness of the world without being dominated by it. She is solitary, a widow, a crone. INTP (Myers-Briggs). She is Libra, the Eagle.

The Queen of Wands – passionate, energetic, profoundly sexual, disturbingly comfortable with her own body to an extent that disconcerts prudes. She sometimes represents athletic prowess and physical strength, and staggering levels of warmth and joy. INTJ (Myers-Briggs). The Queen of Wands is Aries, the Cobra.

THE STAR

People often associate witchcraft with dark or ominous omens. However, one of the most magical of all the tarot cards contradicts that completely. This is the Star, a card which has had a mixed press over the years, with some insisting on seeing it as a symbol of falsity or even deception. However, its magic is the experience of hope, the moment when the bright light of possible transformation dawns and enables us for the first time to recognize that things are really not as bad as all that, that reality is about to turn in our favour. The negative associations probably come from the card's association with the ominous Dog Star, linked to hot summers and outbreaks of diseases, as well as violence. In folklore, it is unlucky to point at a star, or to try to count the stars, and legends report people being struck dead immediately for doing so. Ominous indeed.

But there is beauty to be seen, especially in the Evening Star, the planet Venus. In the Rider–Waite–Smith Tarot, and therefore in most subsequent decks, the Star card shows a naked woman pouring water, giving energy and also correlating hope itself with the acceptance of femininity. The link between the Star and the waters is about tactile connection; and this card, like the Moon and the Sun, partakes of the old system of astrology, in which stars and planets literally transform human beings through their rays. It is as if the woman is bathing in starlight, washed by its serenity.

Thanks to Walt Disney, everybody knows that stars are for wishing. But the tarot card is not about wishes, even though it is occasionally depicted as a shooting star. An older, simpler nursery rhyme offers guidance: "Star light, Star Bright, first star I see tonight. Wish I may, wish I might, get the wish I wish tonight." Then you must be careful not to glimpse your star again, or your wish will be lost. To wish is to believe in hope, to believe that change is possible – and that is magic enough.

HIGH PRIESTESS

A classic and cheering example of the re-paganization of a figure that was once Christian. In early decks, she was Pope Joan, the female Pope. However, in the eighteenth century, she became the High Priestess, the mystical, still virginal guardian of divination itself, and of the path to wisdom. In the Victorian Romantic Tarot, she is a beautiful young witch, standing next to a cauldron. She represents the beauty and desirability of magic itself. The High Priestess is darkness and the unconscious as opposed to rationality. Not specific to women, she represents a part of ourselves which cannot be fully known by thought. She is the potential in our lives which we have yet to fully realize, the half-idea that wakes us in the night, the dream from the beach holiday when we were 17 years old. Not all those ideas might fit with our moral system or our sensible life plans. But the priestess sits on her own throne, bringing a consciousness of what has yet to be made conscious.

WOMEN AND TAROT

The divinatory use of the tarot was transformed by the creation of the Rider-Waite-Smith card deck in 1909. Rider was actually the publisher; the deck was created by mystic Arthur Waite and visual artist Pamela Colman Smith, a member of the hermetic Order of the Golden Dawn, to which she had been introduced by the poet William Butler Yeats. It is Smith's vivid visual designs which remain the basis for the vast majority of tarot decks today, in part because her impressive knowledge of symbolism enabled her to offer clear guidance for card readers. A feminist and campaigner for votes for women, Smith commemorated two of her friends in the cards: the actress Ellen Terry as the Queen of Wands, and Florence Farr – a fellow member of the Order of the Golden Dawn – in the World. Smith herself was the High Priestess, pushed into the shadows and sidelines by the misattribution of the cards to male authors only. But like the High Priestess, her power triumphs – or trumps, perhaps.

DEMETER AND PERSEPHONE

Called Ceres and Proserpina by the Romans, they are mother and daughter, and together they teach us the particular magic of love among change. Demeter stands for stability, our longing for undisturbed lives, the safety and security of routine. Persephone disrupts all that, as children disrupt the assumptions of their parents.

Persephone, the daughter, is the queen of the underworld (hence her alternative name, Praxidike), and ruler of the restless dead. Her return to earth releases the spring and her name is so sacred that she is sometimes just called the girl, Kore. She is abducted by the brother of Zeus, the king of the underworld, Hades. Her mother, Demeter, notices that she is missing, and is informed by Hekate (see page 176) of her daughter's whereabouts. Demeter is the goddess of the grain harvest, and also a mother goddess: her name means mother. Yet in one tale, she is known as Black Demeter, and said to have taken the form of a mare to escape the pursuit of her younger brother, Poseidon. She is raped by him despite her disguise, and then dresses in black and retreats into a cave to mourn and to purify herself.

Yes, these are nature goddesses, but their myths tell the story of the eruption of masculine sexual violence into the lives of women. In the Orphic tradition, while she was searching for her daughter, she was received as a guest by a mortal woman named Baubo, who offered her a meal and wine. Demeter declined because of her grief, but Baubo lifted her skirt and showed her genitalia to the goddess, simultaneously revealing Iacchus, Demeter's son. After that, Demeter was happy.

The Christian era failed to erase mother or daughter. After Theodosius I issued the Edict of Thessalonica and banned paganism throughout the Roman Empire, people throughout Greece continued to pray to Demeter as Saint Demetra, patron saint of agriculture. Around 1765–66, the antiquary Richard Chandler, alongside the architect Nicholas Revett and the painter William Pars, visited Eleusis and mentioned a statue of a caryatid (the draped figure of a woman) as well as the folklore that surrounded it, stating that it was considered sacred by the locals because it protected their crops.

STANDING STONE

Witches have often noticed and used these, and have sometimes been held responsible for their presence in the landscape. Take the Rollright Stones, on the border of Oxfordshire and Warwickshire, supposed to be a group of knights transformed into stone by a witch. The Morrigan, closely associated with witchcraft, was also capable of turning herself into a stone, a feat repeated and mimicked in *The Chronicles of Narnia*, when the White Witch does the same. In Scotland, Carlin Stone is the name given to a number of prehistoric standing stones and natural stone or landscape features; *carlin* is a word for *hag* or *witch*.

Stones could also heal and even embrace. Clach-na-Bhan – Stone of the Woman – near Braemar, Aberdeenshire is an example. Women would journey to this solitary, ancient rock on the top of Clach-na-Bhan in hopes of increasing their chances of an easy childbirth. The rock, which is said to look like an armchair, features a natural hollow that has formed at its centre.

Yet any connection to the past is likely to be a connection to the dead, and especially the restless dead. Agnes Wobster, who was accused of being a witch and who died in 1597, was said to have gone three times to a stone, called the Curstane, at sunrise in May. Cursed stones are also common in Scotland. Five "cursed" stones protect the grave of Seath Mór Sgorfhiaclach in the Doune of Rothiemurchus, and anyone who touches them receives a visit from the Bodach an Duin (the spirit of the Doune). After the stones were associated with several cases of illness and death, an iron grate now keeps them from being touched.

A graveyard on the Isle of Canna was the location of a bullaun stone. This ancient cursing stone was used by Christian pilgrims more than a thousand years ago to bring harm to their enemies. The round stone with an early Christian cross engraved on it would be turned clockwise while praying or when laying a curse, and these were often to be found on Christian pilgrim routes.

Touching stone is touching the past, with all its darkness.

FULL MOON

Everyone understands that this is magical. Constantly referenced in romance from *Romeo and Juliet* to modern love songs, the full moon is a culmination, a ripe fruit. Surprisingly, however, the full moon is less important in Greek and Roman religion than the new moon and the dark moon. Selene, the goddess named for her, is depicted far less often than Artemis and Hekate (see page 176). When the moon is invoked, she is often asked to shed or conceal her light. This becomes less surprising if we recognize the way that magic and the supernatural lie in liminal (transitional) states. The full moon is less magically interesting than the changing moon.

The lunar cycle works as a measurement of time, and thus as a way of coinciding with other parts of nature, whether agrarian, oceanic or celestial. The *Malleus Malificarum* (*Hammer of Witches*) explicitly states that devils particularly molest men at certain phases of the moon, an idea which seems to refer back to the idea of moon madness. In the period of the witch-hunts, witches were supposed to meet when the moon was full. However, this was because the full moon made them mad, and it was believed to be dangerous to sleep in moonlight, especially when the moon is full. *Fool* is a standard pun on *full*, and the moonraker folktale affirms this – fools were said to see the reflection of the moon in a puddle, mistake it for a cheese, and rake the puddle for it.

Moonwort was said to have a strong effect on metal; called into the house, it is also supposed to be capable of unlocking doors. These beliefs might carry a trace of the idea of drawing down the moon.

In some less usual ancient religions, the full moon was connected with immortality – for example, the Mithras Liturgy for eternal life could be performed once a month, at full moon. Ultimately, however, this misrepresents the full moon; though ample, she shines for just a few days, before beginning to wane again, reminding us of our evanescence.

OILS

Oil is central to the religions of the book that have long dominated the West. Often called *chrism*, oil for anointing is important in Christian baptism, the coronations of Christian monarchs, and the last rites administered to the dying. It is the physical representation of the Holy Spirit. A chrism child was an unbaptised child, seen as especially vulnerable to evil magic and to Otherworld powers. It follows that chrism is, among other things, a protection magic that marks out those anointed the way that witch marks protect a house. There is an association between the word *chrism* and the idea of grace – *kharis* in Greek – and charisma. Anointing with oil makes you special.

Oil is also a way of capturing the qualities of plants, as everybody who has ever steeped a chilli in olive or sunflower oil knows. In the twenty-first century, we are much less familiar with the use of oil for light, but that was fundamental to its meaning in the ancient world, where olive oil lamps were much more common than wax candles. Like candles, oil was therefore associated with new ideas, illumination and constancy. Saint Walpurga's dead body exuded a special oil that could be used against witches.

Olive oil in the ancient world was also a precious gift, commonly used to pour out a libation on an altar, or on the earth. This latter practice is a way of looking downwards, towards the spirits and deities below, the spirits of earth and darkness – and that includes the dead. A libation of oil marks out the dead as special, or acknowledges the specialness of the gods. It's also close to the contemporary Latin American practice of bringing a feast to family members' gravesides.

The Greek term for libation, *spondē*, became synonymous with *peace treaty*. Making peace with ourselves might be the best possible uses of oil.

CRYSTAL BALL

The crystal ball is specifically used for two purposes: scrying and clairvoyance. While scrying involves detecting specific messages in a mass of material, such as dreams and visions, clairvoyance – literally, clear seeing – involves seeing people or things that are distant in time or space. This connects with but is not exactly the same as the Scottish idea of second sight.

Dating back to the Roman period, and reported by Pliny the Elder as being used by soothsayers, the crystal ball is connected less with witchcraft than with posh book magic. This is exemplified by Dr John Dee, a mathematician and magician who was an advisor to Elizabeth I. Nobody ever called him a witch. However, people were happy to call him a wizard, in part because of his exceptional understanding of mathematics and geometry. He gathered a huge library of at least 3,000 printed volumes, as well as a large number of manuscripts, housed in his residence at Mortlake. Dee fell in with Edmund Kelley, a con artist who convinced Dee of his own magical abilities, and the pair travelled first to Poland and then to Bohemia. Returning to England, Dee found his home and library vandalized.

The procedure for scrying was that Dee and his medium would retire to a private room where a crystal was set up. There Dee sat in a corner with pen and paper, ready to record the answers to his questions. The medium knelt before the crystal and reported on what he saw and heard in it. The spirits who appeared included the archangels Uriel, Michael and Raphael, and a little girl called Madimi, who could be terrifyingly moody. While Dee's manuscripts survive, they are written in an angelic language which only he understood.

In both medieval and Tudor times, scrying was most often done with any shiny surface, rather than specifically with a crystal ball. A mirror would do. Dee's Speculum or Mirror is an obsidian Aztec cult object in the shape of a hand mirror, brought to Europe in the late 1520s. It was subsequently owned by Horace Walpole, who was the first to attribute it to Dee. Lord Frederick Campbell had brought "a round piece of shining black marble in a leathern case" to Walpole in an attempt to ascertain its provenance. Walpole said he responded saying, "Oh, Lord, I am the only man in England that can tell you! It is Dr Dee's black stone".

COME, BUTTER, COME;
COME, BUTTER, COME.
PETER STANDS AT THE GATE
WAITING FOR A BUTTER CAKE;
COME, BUTTER, COME.

DASH CHURN

A lot of cooking is magic, transforming inedible substances into food. Every woman who could read and write used to keep a book of recipes that included both healing potions and recipes for food. The magic of preservation was especially important in a period before refrigeration.

Cheese and butter were vital foods in the diet of the poor, because they offered fat – often considered bad now, but essential for life in small quantities. Churning butter was an especially important task, a kind of portable magic, with the dash churn – like a mortar and pestle – symbolically representing the power of the human body. Without any machinery, it was the physical strength of the woman herself that transformed cream into something that would keep for months.

Churning was a fickle and tricky process. If it didn't work, women invoked charms to coax the butter out of the cream, such as this charm opposite.

It's almost like a love charm, calling the butter like a pet like a Familiar (see page 154). The charm used to say *Saint* Peter, but Protestants saw the naming of a saint as wicked paganism; they didn't like the implication that a butter cake might be a way through the gates of heaven. The steady, pounding rhythm required to make butter with a dash churn is also sexual, fertile.

If the butter didn't come, people might say that there was a witch in the churn, taking control away from the woman who wanted butter. A cleansing spell could put things right; typically, this involved fire, putting a hot metal object like a poker into the churn to make it pure and clean.

When we transform a substance, we feel our own power over nature in arms, in our hands. When we share what we have made with others, we build a magical community. When we make our homes into a safe and delicious space, we experience a magical delight known to woman for centuries. That power, like other powers, can be transferred to enable us to feel at home in our bodies and to welcome others without fear.

INCENSE BURNER

In the history of magic, smell is underrated in comparison with touch and sight. Yet smell is a vital part of ourselves, and it is essential to our sense of home, which in turn is a crucial part of witch identity. Our houses have to smell right. What is right for one person may be alien to another. The right smell often requires maintenance, and sometimes can require a ritual to take back a space.

Burning incense is a perfect example of that. It is also a way of attracting and honouring otherworldly beings in many Western religions. This may date back to the cult of the Egyptian goddess Isis, immensely popular in ancient Rome. Satisfyingly exotic and magical, Isis had dealings with the dead and care for the dead, and she especially appreciated the gift of rich perfumed incense, used in the mummification and preservation of the dead. Incense is also a way of inhaling and incorporating a remedy.

The ancient world especially favoured spikenard, or nard, now a critically endangered plant, but once a precious resource from the desert. Another ancient incense is *Boswellia*, called frankincense or olibanum: the incense is made by making a cut in the bark of the plant, and the sap exuded from it is called its tears. It is a powerful anti-inflammatory, used today to treat joint pain.

Any aromatic material can be used to make incense if ground in a mortar and pestle (see page 160) with a gum resin. Lists of ingredients used for incense read like poems: cardamom, cassia, cedar, cinnamon, myrrh, opoponax, patchouli, sandalwood, vetiver... The grind must be very fine so that the material can be caked together for quick burning – in the words of the poet Alexander Pope, "all Arabia breathes from yonder box".... Like the Silk Road, the Incense Route was a thousand-mile network of trade routes for the passage of caravans carrying incense and myrrh. The lost incense city of Ubar, an important trading post, was nicknamed Atlantis of the Sands by Lawrence of Arabia, and is also called Iram of the Pillars; archaeologists claimed to have rediscovered it in the 1990s, but the claim is contested. When you burn incense, remember the city.

SICKLE MOON

The time to begin. In astrology and in witchcraft, any project begun under a sickle moon will grow and swell with the powers of the waxing moon. For many centuries, people have chosen to work with the lunar tide in every aspect of their lives, but especially with relation to the growing year. The new moon is the time to sow seeds. Just as ships in the Age of Sail had to wait for the tide, which meant waiting for the moon, farmers also had to coordinate with strong and cosmic forces. In the twenty-first century, commerce is uncomfortable even with holidays set by lunar months (Easter, Ramadan, Passover), but such holidays are holy days indeed, because they remind us that all of us are sublunary creatures, and subject to forces outside the daily grind.

In thinking this way, witches can also reconnect with ancient religious traditions. The ancient Greeks celebrated Noumenia when the first sliver of moon was visible, to honour Selene, Apollon Noumenios, Hestia and the other Hellenic household gods. The day before – the eve of the feast – is a scary liminal time. Hekate's Deipnon is the last day before the first slice of visible moon and the last day in a lunar month, while Noumenia marks the first day in a lunar month, and is followed by the Agathos Daimon (Good Spirit) on the second day of the lunar month. (Note Halloween, All Saints' Day, All Souls' Day – exactly the same pattern.) It was a day of relaxation and feasting for Athenian citizens, at home; like the Jews after the diaspora, and modern Catholics, ancient Greeks practised much of their religion at home. The City of Athens also made a small offering to the magical snake, which they believed to be a new form of their mythical king Kekrops.

WELL

When we think of wishing wells now, we usually think of modern fakes. But a wishing well is a traditional site of power, and there are very many that have been in use for hundreds of years. Often, wells were repurposed to Christian legends – for example, the famous Treacle Well in the churchyard of Binsey was associated with Saint Margaret, the patroness of women in childbirth, and one ritual connected with it involved dipping the girdle of the pregnant woman in the well, almost certainly a hangover from ancient times. The so-called Chalice Well at Glastonbury is another well-known example. Still other wells offered healing or omens. In that sense, all wells are wishing wells. For many centuries before the custom of dropping coins in a well emerged, people would make wishes in a ritualistic fashion – while dropping pebbles or coins in silence at midnight, or while drinking water from the other hand at the same time. The ancient springs at Bath were used to drop curses rather than wishes.

This is witchcraft, but where are the witches? In Scotland, the Cailleach Bheur, or Old Hag of the Ridges, was the guardian of a fountain that welled up from the peak of Ben Cruachan. Beira was a one-eyed giantess with white hair, dark blue skin and rust-coloured teeth. She built the mountains of Scotland using a magic hammer. The longest night of the year marked the end of her reign as Queen of Winter, at which time she visited the Well of Youth and, after drinking its magic water, grew younger day by day.

There is a tale of five brothers, who go hunting and lose their way in the woods. They decide to camp for the night and go searching for water. Each of them meets an old woman guarding a well, and she asks them to sleep with her. When Niall approaches her, he kisses her and is prepared to lie with her, at which point she turns into a beautiful woman. Tales like this where use of a well is linked to a new destiny may explain the way Scottish witches sometimes used wells as methods of divination.

VENUS/HOLDA

From caves to old stones, witches have always sought safe and secret spaces. Such spaces are often inhabited by otherworldly beings, and the Venusberg is one example. When the minstrel and singer Tannhauser disappeared, he was said to have gone to the Venusberg (the Venus Mountain, inside which is a deep cave) to consort with Venus, just as Thomas the Rhymer went to fairyland to be with the Queen of the Fairies. Both realms are deep in the earth, and both men emerge with the gift of powerful song. The stories of both has been Christianized, so that the underground realm of pleasure becomes a hellscape. But Venus may also be another name for Holda, also called Mother Holly (see Tree, page 98). When girls visit her, they are granted a knowledge of the fertility of the land, and of household management. The ability to manage winter is a near magical capability in northern Europe. Holda may also be Perchta (see page 120), and she is also referenced in the same ninth-century sources that reference the women who ride with the goddess Diana:

> Have you believed there is some female, whom the stupid vulgar call Holda... who is able to do a certain thing, such that those deceived by the devil affirm themselves by necessity and by command to be required to do, that is, with a crowd of demons transformed into the likeness of women, on fixed nights to be required to ride upon certain beasts, and to themselves be numbered in their company?

> These female figures are also connected with both singing and spinning. They give the gift of knowledge to their followers, and a visit to their realm followed by a return to human life allows visitors to take that knowledge and power back to human societies. Often, their followers return to that Otherworld at the end.

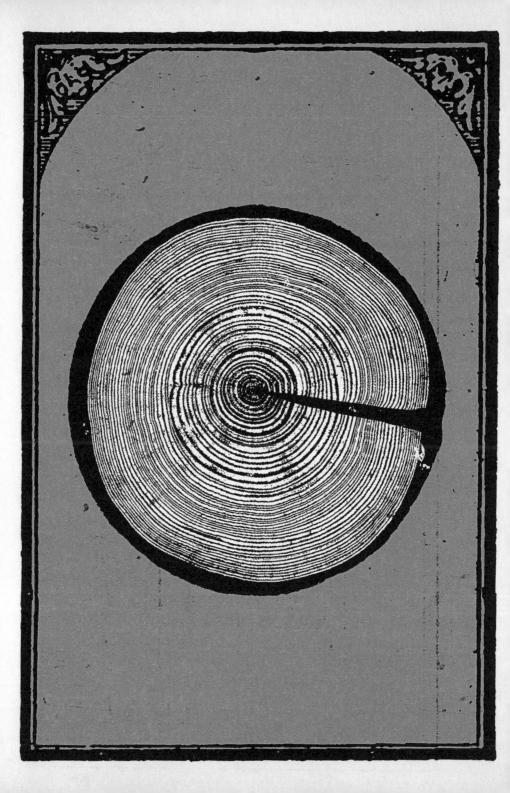

WOOD

Wood is, if you think about it, the cadaver of a tree, or the severed limb of one. Part of witchcraft is understanding the things we hide from ourselves. That shouldn't make for despair, but for gratitude and a sense of connection. But the word *wood* also refers to an area of land covered with trees. In fairy tales, such spaces are often scary – they are framed as the home of fierce animals, such as wolves, and also as a likely space to find a witch. That's what happens to Hansel and Gretel, or so we are told. The witch gets all the blame, and is herself a frightening predator. Yet this story encloses fragments of older stories. When the Brothers Grimm originally collected the tale, they called it "The children in time of famine", and it describes how the children's biological mother wants to eat them when the bread runs out. The Grimms transferred that idea onto somebody other than the mother, and that's what the witch is – the parts of the mother that we as a society cannot stand or tolerate.

Actually, the witch is initially helpful, although this is framed as duplicitous. She makes apple pancakes for the starving children. Many accusations from the time of the witch trials involve witches giving food to children, an action seen as sinister because only the mother is supposed to provide food and knowledge. To feed a child is an act of usurpation. But the witch you meet in the wood might have the power you need, as the story of Baba Yaga shows. Her wood is dark and deadly, her house marked by skulls on sticks, but she can help those who respect her power – and she does. In folklore, therefore, a journey through a dark wood is the beginning of change, an act that shows a commitment to change our lives for the better.

What do witches bring back from that dark wood? Among other things, they bring back wood itself, which gives light and heat, symbolizing knowledge and comfort. The Witch of Edmonton, Elizabeth Sawyer, is initially attacked just for gathering wood for fuel; she was executed in 1621.

THE HORSEMAN'S WORD

Many believed in a witch's ability to control horses in mysterious and magical ways, reputedly by whispering a secret word into the animal's ear. In particular, they claimed they could handle any horse and make it come to them ("drawing" the horse) or more spectacularly could reduce a horse to immobility ("jading" it), which no power on earth could shift until the controlling horseman himself released it.

A toadman or toad-man is someone who, in the folklore of the Fens of East Anglia and Lincolnshire, has made a deal with the devil which gives them control over horses. He needed a particular breed of toad (the natterjack, or *Bufo calamita*, according to some). This was killed and hung on a whitethorn bush for 24 hours to dry, and then buried for a month in an anthill to remove the flesh. At the next full moon, the skeleton was placed in a running stream, and the would-be toadman watched carefully for one particular bone to float upstream. The participant was warned to ignore the terrible noises that would occur just behind him – on no account looking round, or risk losing the power. The special bone was then taken home, treated with particular oils, baked and powdered, and this then gave the bearer power over horses (and, in some versions, pigs and women).

Evans also describes an alternative preparation based on the milt, which is an oval-shaped lump of fibrous matter found in a foal's mouth immediately after it is born. The ritual convinced the horsemen that they were dealing with evil powers or the devil himself – and was used by them to impress others – and thus the power they gained was both mysterious and dangerous, and their own reputation as horse-handlers was enhanced.

Toads are generally portrayed in negative terms in Western culture, and are often associated with witches, but here, the sacrifice of the toad confers supernatural power over nature and is almost entirely positive. This is, however, another example of the use of bodies and flesh in magic, and even of animal sacrifice.

TREE

Like standing stones and caves, trees are permanent, and therefore tend to represent eternity. All trees are magical, but in Western Europe, three are more magical than others: ash, oak and thorn.

Oak is ancient, and a storied tree across Europe. Thor, a Norse god, was related to lightning storms, strength and the oak. The oak's magic powers could bring good luck, financial success and fertility. Individual trees therefore pick up legends and tales of their own, such as the oak tree in Windsor Great Park, associated with the wild hunt led by Herne the Hunter. The ash tree is the second in the sacred trio. In Norse mythology the Tree of Life, Yggdrasil, which held the nine worlds of the cosmos, is an ash.

But what was thorn? Some say holly, used to protect the home from malevolent faeries. Some modern pagans say the Holly King rules from the summer to the winter solstice, when the Oak King defeats the Holly King to rule until the summer solstice again. Putting hollies in hedges obstructed witches who people believed ran along the tops of hedges. However, Mother Holly (Holle) is a witch figure. Others say *thorn* is hawthorn. The Glastonbury Thorn was a hawthorn that flowers twice a year; it grew where Joseph of Arimathea visited Glastonbury with the Holy Grail and thrust his staff into Wearyall Hill. The thorn is first mentioned in a pamphlet published by Richard Pynson in 1520; it was a sign of divine favour, proof that Glastonbury was "the holyest erth of Englande".

Yet there is another tree associated with magic, the yew tree, associated with death and the journey of the soul from this life to the next for thousands of years, and said to be sacred to Hekate (see page 176). Many of the ancient yew trees in churchyards predate Christianity; the church and the churchyard grew up on a pagan site. The yew's poisons were believed to come from the vapours escaping from the graves. The witches in Shakespeare's *Macbeth* use "slips of yew, silvered in the moon's eclipse" to create a prophecy magic.

CLEFT IN THE EARTH

At Creswell Crags, a limestone gorge on the Nottinghamshire–Derbyshire border with a history dating back 60,000 years, thousands of witch marks (see pages 30 and 32) have been discovered carved into walls and ceilings of the caves, over dark holes and large crevices.

The number and variety of designs for witch marks is unprecedented. Among the most common found are the double VV engravings which are believed to make reference to Mary, Virgin of Virgins; similarly, PM references Pace Maria. Work on folklore has suggested that in some parts of Europe, rituals connected with the Virgin Mary were once associated with pagan goddesses, although we probably don't want to say this was always so. Nevertheless, in the ballad of Thomas the Rhymer, Thomas does mistake the Queen of the Fairies for the Virgin Mary...

In the ancient world, even epic heroes had to undergo *katabasis*, the going downwards into darkness to search for the ultimate truth about death and the dead. As children, many of us longed to find secret passages and tunnels in the earth, and there are hundreds of them in the British Isles, such as Lud's Church in the Peak District, cool and damp even on the hottest days, Thor's Cave at Wetton, and the abandoned copper mines on Alderley Edge. Many legends are associated with these empty spaces, even if some are man-made. It seems that we need to populate such landscapes with tales of adventure and heroism, and also to read them as portals, entrances to another world from which spirits might come, or through which humans might go into a different time. In such spaces, King Arthur waits until he is needed; dragons also lurk beneath the surface.

While it is always magical in the best sense to follow others along paths they have already trodden to such crafts between worlds, it is always open to us as individuals to find our own spaces, even if they are just wardrobes – and who knows where a wardrobe might lead, especially if we keep our books there?

Of course, cleft spaces also suggest female genitalia. And why should they not be magic?

FIRE

Of the four elements, fire is the one with the claims to bring civilization in its wake. It is by cooking food that we increase its power to fuel our bodies; it is by heating metal that we bend it to our will. Yet fire is also part of the magic that can hurt the one who wishes to use it; our bodies are vulnerable to it, and the ultimate fate of witches in most of Europe illustrates the shared belief that the body of the witch must be destroyed in fire to be disempowered. The power of fire to cleanse can also become its power to destroy. Rituals involving fire are usually about cleansing but can also be about acts of destruction.

Paracelsus characterized the fire elemental as a salamander. Lean, flexible and capable of living in the fire as its natural home, the salamander embodies the power of fire. Zodiac signs are also characterized through the four elements: the fire signs are Aries, Leo and Sagittarius, and they are like fire itself – brilliant, shining, but also burning too hot, subject to bursts of rage and passion. In tarot, the Suit of Wands is ruled by fire – fast, energetic, hard to control. Fire can be mobile, uncontrollable. And it can be frightening, especially in the modern world we have made.

One man who witnessed the first atomic bomb detonation at Los Alamos described what he saw: "The whole country was lighted by a searing light with the intensity many times that of the midday sun. It was golden, purple, violet, gray, and blue. It lighted every peak, crevasse, and ridge of the nearby mountain range with a clarity and beauty that cannot be described but must be seen to be imagined...like the end of the world." Ever since, the small flame of a household candle has had the power to evoke this far greater burst of agonizing flame.

HOLLOW WAY

The old countries of Europe are full of secrets. For people who are themselves part of European cultures, but who live in countries that were recently established through colonialism, such as the settler colonies of the United States, Australia and New Zealand, the constant presence of European antiquity in the landscape of European countries can appear especially seductive as an almost visible link to the past. A perfectly ordinary graveyard in Gloucestershire can conceal under your feet a Roman mosaic. And even that is a johnny-come-lately in comparison with the really ancient roads of the British Isles.

Oldest of all is the Ridgeway, an ancient trackway extending from Wiltshire along the chalk ridge of the Berkshire Downs to the River Thames at the Goring Gap. It is part of the Icknield Way which ran, not always on the ridge, from Salisbury Plain to East Anglia. Henry of Huntingdon wrote that the Ermine Street, Fosse Way, Watling Street and Icknield Way were constructed by royal authority, but the first three of these are in part Roman creations and the last pre-Roman.

The passage of feet over centuries changes the landscape. A hollow way is a shaded, sometimes enclosed path which can be as much as 5.5m (18ft) beneath the level of fields, worn down, as Robert Macfarlane observes, by traffic and the action of water. They are the result of repeated human actions, like creases in a human hand, or a worn doorstep or stair. The old hollow ways still connect to other old paths and tracks, linking places and people. If witches walk the lines of nature's palm, then they walk the ancient darkness too.

Some of the old trackways are associated with a figure who may once have been a goddess or a witch. This is Helen of the Roads, said to have ordered the making of Sarn Helen, the great Roman road running through Wales. Though this road bears her name, it is considerably older than the accepted time period for Helen. Yet travellers are still under her protection.

FREYJA

The word in Old Norse simply means *lady*. It's not a name, but a refusal to say a specific name, and that in itself suggests the magical associations of this particular deity. Just as people are traditionally very reluctant to say the word *fairy*, preferring instead to use euphemisms such as *our good neighbours*, so referring to a deity in a roundabout fashion marks a cautious space. And there is reason for caution: Freyja may be the most powerful goddess in any Western mythology, and one who is strongly associated with magic.

Freyja is the ultimate *völva*, which is a particular kind of seer, who practises *seidr* – the art of discerning the fate of individuals, and weaving new fates for them (see Weaving, Knotting, Wicca, page 122). The *seidr* power could potentially be put to any use imaginable, and examples that cover virtually the entire range of the human condition can be found in Old Norse literature. Daniel McCoy explains that the *völva* was a travelling magic-user from whom acts of magic – *seidr* – could be requested, and paid for with food or a room for the night. Her clients might long for her to visit, but they might be terrified when she did.

Sounds exactly like a witch...

But she is also a goddess.

Archaeologist Neil Price shows that she represents every aspect of the lives of women. And she is always in control, regardless of attempts by gods, dwarves, giants and others to objectify or coerce her. She takes lovers as she chooses. Significantly, she drives a wagon pulled by cats, and she is as untameable as they are. She can use sex work as a political weapon: efforts to slut-shame her have no effect on her self-esteem. Yet she is also a deity of the battlefield. The Viking warrior dead go to her as well as to Valhalla. Her power to control cats (see page 146) may be the origin of the witch's cat, and she also makes use of a magical staff, like that associated with wizards.

ZODIAC

Over our heads is a great ribbon of constellations, turning like a great wheel. These are twelve signs, pictures made of stars, and the sun makes its way through all of them in turn. All right, it's not really like that, because the whole idea comes from a time when we believed that the sun went around the earth, but the zodiac remains relevant to us because it's an analysis of how we cannot help but see the universe. For us, from our earthbound point of view, the sun moves through and around the zodiac.

Many centuries ago, it was believed that stars and planets literally transformed the beings and substances touched by their rays. Actually, this is scientifically true – the rays of the sun really do transform skin, hair, plants, the surface of the sea, and everything else they touch. The movement of the moon really does create tides. Extrapolating from this, astronomers used to believe that the rays of the sun created gold; the rays of Venus created copper in the soil; the rays of the moon, silver; the rays of Mars, iron; and so on. This in turn was a model for the effect of stars and planets on the lives of human beings – we still speak of a *golden opportunity*, which might be something created by a conjunction between the sun and another planet.

In the time of the witchcraft persecutions, it was forbidden to cast the horoscope of the monarch in case it became possible to pick out unlucky days for him on which a rebellion could take place. While we don't know if witches directly used astrology, as opposed to the many other ways they had of predicting the future or discovering secrets, it's possible to imagine that the widespread presence of the almanac – a calendar with astronomical details – meant that most people were familiar with the idea of the movements of the planets affecting growth and luck; a "zodiacal body" mapping the influence of the planets on body parts and organs. It was a way of understanding the place of the body in the universe.

BOOK OF SHADOWS

Specifically, the term used for the magical grimoire (see also Grimoire, page 172) created by Gerald Gardner, and used by him in his first coven, but now a general term for a Modern Pagan or Wiccan book of magic.

Gardner created British traditional witchcraft using the historical work of Margaret Murray, and accepting her now discredited theory that the witches of the past worshipped a mother goddess and a male god of wild nature. As a result, much of his book of shadows concerns religious rituals. Any consensus about the identity of these deities has been difficult to sustain in the face of the remarkable self-taught knowledge and inventiveness of the modern pagan community. For example, the male god is now commonly interpreted as, for instance, death, or the eternally rivalrous Oak King and Holly King, while the goddess is often understood not only as Gaia, the living Earth, and the triple goddess of the three phases of the moon, but also as change and transformation. Central to books of shadows is the charge of the goddess, which exists in many forms: here is one example.

Listen to the words of the Great Mother, who was of old also called Artemis; Astarte; Diana; Melusine; Aphrodite; Cerridwen; Dana; Arianrhod; Isis; and Bride. She was also known by many other names:

Whenever you have need or seek to offer thanks, once in the month, and better when the moon is full, seek out some secret place and adore the spirit of Me who is Queen of all the Wise. In this place shall I share with you the Secret Wisdom of the Ages. You shall be free from self-bondage, and as a sign that you be free you shall be naked in your rites, in your mind. Sing, feast, dance, make merry, make music and love, all in My presence, for Mine is the ecstasy of the spirit and Mine also is joy on Earth... Mine is the secret door that opens upon the door of youth, and Mine is the cup of the Wine Of Life that is the Cauldron of Cerridwen – the holy grail of immortality.

DARK MOON

In a nutshell, the moonless night symbolizes death, sexuality and the unconscious. In Christian cosmology, the region below the moon is imperfect. It's sublunary, out of touch with God, rebellious and ungovernable, and out of tune with the music of the spheres. In Dante's *Divine Comedy*, the sphere of the moon is the Heaven for those who have loved too greatly (but not sinfully).

These are the natural dwelling places of witches, and that is why the dark moon especially is associated with black magic. However, if we fail to notice our own dark sides, and simply squash them, how can we hope for any real power?

In the Fen Country, there is a story about the moon dying one day; the time came for the new moon to be born, and the sky remained dark. The Fenlanders could no longer cross the fens because they needed the illumination the moon provided to stop themselves from falling into a marsh and drowning. Then, a Fenlander discovered the moon imprisoned by the wicked spirits of the fens (called bogies). They were hoping for more human prey in her absence. Once released, she soared back into the heavens.

The story illustrates how and why the dark moon frightened our ancestors. Before reliable artificial illumination, human beings were dependent on the lights provided by nature. A candle provides exactly as much light as a fridge bulb, and for many centuries, ordinary people could not afford large and expensive lamps, or multiple candles. Yet they had tasks that had to be performed, often in landscapes rich in dangers. They could organize those tasks around the lunar cycle, but it was understandable to fear the darkness and to fear even more that the darkness might be permanent, that the moon could be used up or devoured, gone forever. She was always understood as wayward, wilful, inconstant, unreliable. Of course she was; she wasn't always there. Her absence dominates the other ways we think about her presence; we know she will not always be with us, which is why we celebrate her return and fear her loss.

STONE CIRCLE

Many witches in the British Isles developed their craft in a particular landscape, one where an inscrutable past is visible in ancient barrows, stone circles and, in Scotland, Pictish stones. Witches understood those stones in their own way. In 1597, Margaret Bane and Margaret Og were seen dancing around a great stone on Halloween, a nameless stone beneath Craigleauch in Deeside. Bane was also seen throwing water and earth and stone (a ritual of land ownership) over her shoulders. The Puritans interrogating these women saw dancing as a sure sign of sinful pleasure, but the women may have seen it as a way into an Otherworld. Sir Walter Scott notes that in some parts of Scotland: "It is believed...that if, on Hallowe'en, any person, alone, goes round one of these hills nine times, towards the left hand ... a door shall be opened by which he shall be admitted into their subterranean abodes." The Edinburgh witch Elizabeth Dunlop describes entering the fairy Otherworld through an ancient stone gateway.

Circling around a stone or stone circle is linked to attempts to rescue the fairy-taken. To free his sister, Childe Rowland is told to go on until he comes to "a round green hill surrounded with rings from the bottom to the top; go round it three times widershins, and every time say, 'Open, door! open, door! and let me come in'; and the third time the door will open, and you may go in." Childe Rowland is mentioned in Shakespeare's *King Lear*, and although the ballad survives only in fragments, a folktale version exists, which may or may not be based on the ballad and perhaps even on the play. This version locates the story at the court of King Arthur, also evoked in connection with other stones and wells.

The fear evoked by these remains explains why many still exist today, for it was said that spirits resented human interference with the stone circle. Many tales told of men removing the stones only to be punished with mishaps. This left the stones in place, as gateways to magic.

COVEN

In the time of the witch trials, only the prosecutors insisted that witches worked together in large groups and met for frequent sabbats. The word *coven* is simply a variant of the word *convent*, and means an assembly of any kind. Promulgated by the twentieth-century anthropologist Margaret Murray, the word is used in just one Scottish witchcraft trial, by Isobel Gowdie, who confessed in 1662 that there were 13 people in each coven, a claim that was repeated by Anne Armstrong in Northumbria in 1673, also speaking of *coveys* of 13. Both these women were so extraordinary that it would be a mistake to regard anything they said as typical. It was Sir Walter Scott who picked up the word in his century *Letters on Demonology and Witchcraft* (1830), and the idea was further promulgated by Margaret Murray, as part of her thesis that the trial records witches meeting in groups of 13. This information turned out to be wrong, in that Murray had changed the sources to achieve the desired number.

Rather than thinking of covens, then, we should probably think of witchcraft as characterized by solitary practitioners who sometimes form loose associations with one another to perform particular actions in particular places, such as the circling, dancing witches recorded in some Scottish witch trials. Like much else about witchcraft that has passed into popular culture, the idea of the coven is an idea created by the enemies of witches, not by witches themselves.

TALISMAN

An object that brings good luck or repels bad luck, or the evil eye, and so not very different from an amulet. In many cultures, talismans are fetishes – that is, parts of something larger (such as a rabbit's foot). The Portuguese *feitiço*, meaning *spell*, comes from the Latin *factitius*, itself from *facere*, to do, or to make, and signifies something made by art.

The term *fetish* was used contemptuously for African magical practices, but it simply means carrying a large amount of energy and magic with you by carrying a token, symbol or image – and that is something that most of us do in daily life, whether it is our lucky exam pen, a special medallion in the car, or a lock of hair taken from the head of somebody dear to us. In a way, all those things are magic because all of them make a connection. When we carry a talisman, we connect with something larger.

Much energy and ink has been expended talking about the kind of power that lies in an object like this. Is it some kind of animism, in which a material item is filled with the power of a particular spirit, or is it some kind of infusion of the material with the spiritual, conducted by ritual? We might respond: "Who knows and who cares?" Every society on earth has practices of this kind. The question might be why they continue in an age where Western culture has developed personal insurance, say, to work against bad luck – which the historian Keith Thomas thinks is the answer to belief in witchcraft.

The answer is the basic human understanding that, regardless of insurance, good and bad luck are still important. But there is a separate and darker answer, which is that since the beginning of human society, people have hoped that there is a way to buy good luck, and to sell the idea of good luck to other people. While it is fair to pay somebody for their labour in making a jewel, the old rule that magic itself can never be bought or sold is worth remembering.

THE SNOW QUEEN

Is she a witch or a goddess? She seems simply to represent the snow itself, in its exquisite beauty and power, its hidden mathematics and geometry, its cool logic and intellect. A.S. Byatt writes about her identification with the Snow Queen as a woman allowed both beauty and intelligence, a refuge from a world where women are simply domestic figures. Hans Andersen himself said he was haunted by an icewoman who represented death, and his father said she had come to fetch him. The Snow Queen is also the magic of adolescence, the point where we want to put away childish things and feelings to embrace other possibilities. She also carries with her the trace of mist lands, the realm of ice and snow, the land of the dead, ruled over by Hel, the Queen of Death (related to Mother Holle of German folklore).

While the story wants us to discard the Snow Queen, it's the kind of story which invites truculent misreading. In Emma Donoghue's retelling, it is Gerda who is invited into the Snow Queen's Palace, and the way to it even in the original is guarded by genuine "Lapland" witches, themselves emblems of the cold North and the indigenous peoples who were at home in it and therefore persecuted as witches.

The Sami people were regarded with fear and hatred because of their pagan and magical beliefs. "Sami witchcraft should be persecuted without mercy," said King Christian IV of Denmark and Norway in 1609. The law used the Old Norse term of *trolldomr*. In the Finnmark trials, 37 Sami were convicted, and 25 executed. This is part of the origin for the White Witch in *The Chronicles of Narnia*, an outsider, not fully human, and therefore evil.

Later Snow Queens transmute their icy magic into art. In the Disney film *Frozen*, Elsa escapes into a world where her magic can explode into the creation of a beautiful castle made of song and ice. Of course, she is not allowed to live there, because the film wants her to be reintegrated into the family, but if Elsa were a witch, she would stay on.

WEAVING, KNOTTING, WICCA

Most magic involves binding, knotting. Or, conversely, it can involve loosening and untying. Take the magic used by Scottish witches to safeguard the house every quarter day; they took branches of a rowan tree, and tied them with red thread, placing them near thresholds and windows. An old rhyme says: "Rowan-tree and red thread,/ Put the witches to their speed" – that is, send the witches away. This small domestic magic of knotting and tying is also fundamental to many other kinds of binding spell, but it also links to much larger and more powerful magic users, through the image of spinning and weaving as more comprehensive kinds of knotting. The lives of human beings are also woven and spun, by figures who are almost always female in the traditions of Western Europe. Perhaps the most terrifying are the Valkyries. In the poem "Darraðarljóð" in the medieval Icelandic *Njal's Saga*, we see them standing before a loom on which they have woven a cloth from the intestines of dead men while using human heads as loom weights. This makes literal what it means to be a weaver of the fates of men on the field of battle. The tricoteuses, old women who knitted at the foot of the guillotine as the heads of aristocrats were severed from their bodies during the French Revolution, retain a faint trace of such power.

It used to be believed that the very word *witch* derived from a word that meant *weaving*, an idea which strongly appealed to Gerald Gardner because it implied continuity with pre-Christian religious practices of Anglo-Saxon England. However, more recent research suggests that the word witchcraft simply comes from Anglo-Saxon *wiccecraeft*. But what exactly was *the craft* in question? A craft always involves making things by hand, but can also be a description of something deceptive. Perhaps this craft brought things together, knotted them together, made them entangled with one another.

ATHAME

A double-edged knife, typically having a black handle, used for ritual purposes in Wicca and other modern pagan movements. The first usage of the term is recorded in 1931, in the *Oxford English Dictionary*: "She is moving with a regal gait, grasping the arthame, or magic knife." Note that it is spelled differently.

While many modern pagan texts will say that the origin of the word is unknown, the *Oxford English Dictionary* offers a cogent account of its early usage, in an eighteenth-century manuscript of a text on witchcraft, the *Key of Solomon*, also known as the *Clavicula* (see Grimoire, page 172). It would be wrong to see this as a book; it's more of a format into which individuals have inserted their own rituals and interpretations, leading to a confusion of different manuscripts. One such manuscript contains a medieval French term for *cutting*, and this may be the origin of the word.

Whenever you set out to invent a religion, it's a good idea to behave like a fantasy writer. Inventing recondite terms that sound ancient lends substance. That is what both Aleister Crowley and Gerald Gardner did to create the identity of the modern witch. (Yes, modern witchcraft was invented by two men, although women have reinvented it many times since then.)

Both Crowley and Gardner were conceptually indebted to the great syncretic mythographers of the nineteenth century such as James George Frazer, and the equally syncretic religious practices of the Theosophical Society. Many of the assumptions of these groups don't sit particularly well with the values of the twenty-first century, not least Crowley's regalia, partially adopted by Gardner: sword, dagger, wand, censer, pentacle and scourge. (The symbol of the cup, familiar from tarot, does not appear, leaving some rather phallic-looking materials in its place.)

In his important account of Gardner's intellectual development, Ronald Hutton writes about his interest in ancient Cypriot metalwork and his preoccupation with the magical associations of swords and daggers. Like everything else in modern paganism, the athame is an invention, and everybody is free to choose whether it makes sense to them – or not.

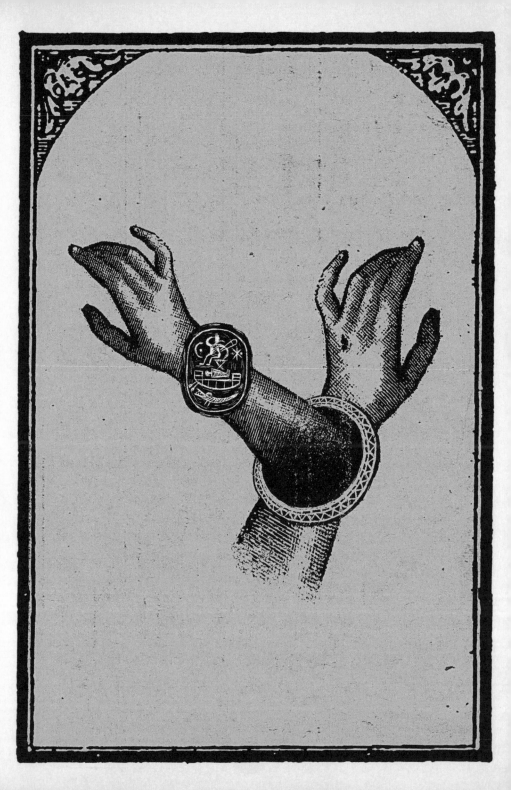

AMULET

Any magically potent object worn for protection against witchcraft, illness, the evil eye or accidents, or to bring luck or love, can be an amulet.

Amulets can be made of stone, flesh, bone or plants. The body parts of those who died a violent death, such as executed criminals or victims of shipwreck, are particularly helpful. There is no need for expensive precious stones or metals, though those do have magical properties – so use pressed flowers, withered leaves or a bag of earth from your garden. Be guided by your feelings.

Here is a formula for an amulet. Write a powerful name. The most useful is a name that's completely unfamiliar to you and the people around you, and here it's good to use an unknown alphabet as well. Next write some magic words, typically nonsense words like *abracadabra*, and then explain what you want to push away from you – "Sickness, be off", "Pain, be gone" – or what you want to attract – "Luck, come to me." Look elsewhere in this book for some magic things and magical names you can use.

ROBES

At Halloween, ideas about what witches wear can be seen on every street corner. Black and ragged clothing predominates. By contrast, those modern pagans who derive their practices from the Druids often adopt druid garments, which are highly symbolical and mostly date from the nineteenth century's reimagining of the ancient Druids.

There's absolutely no harm in ceremonial dressing for ritual. Like most kinds of magic, it's a way of building from the outside in; and making something inside yourself often begins with playing a part, which in turn involves costume and make-up, and the business of putting them on as a way of changing from being a ordinary person to being a person doing something extraordinary. Some images of beautiful witches created in the nineteenth century show them wearing luscious and sensuous silks and furs. Enviable – but not what witches have always done.

In the early days of modern paganism, witches liked to work sky-clad – naked – because Gerald Gardner was a keen naturist and connected body acceptance with nudity and with casting off the trappings of culture. In visual art, witches of the past are often portrayed naked. However, these portrayals are meant to demean them, to show them as ugly, shameless or sexual – something that a modern witch might want to reflect on and then reclaim.

Conversely, witches might choose to work wearing what they are comfortable wearing, whatever that is. Just as there is power in noticing clothes, there is a different kind of power in refusing to think endlessly about self-presentation. Do as you will.

STORM

However much we have equipment that allows us to predict them now, a really first-class storm still feels like angry weather. When Sir Francis Drake had just begun his circumnavigation of the world, he ran into a very sudden storm on the Atlantic coast of Argentina, a kind of storm the locals call *pompano*. Drake and his chaplain immediately assumed there was witchcraft afoot, and one of the expedition was later hanged for conniving with indigenous peoples to create the storm. This disturbing anecdote illustrates how strongly bad weather was linked with witchcraft. It has even been argued that one of the causes of witchcraft persecutions was the Little Ice Age, a drop in temperature averaging 1.5°C across the region of the North Atlantic, which, like the current climate emergency, created more extreme weather events, including huge storms. Accusations of weather magic were among the most common in the period of the witch trials, especially in Europe.

Those at sea in ships were especially vulnerable. Yet many fishermen used magic and rituals to call up a good wind, and sometimes their powers were thought to have run amok. The most famous example of witches causing storms concerns James VI of Scotland. Witches were said to have flung cats into the ocean in order to raise a storm to prevent James from reaching his bride in Norway; Norwegian and Danish witches were also said to have been involved. The storm was also considered a treasonable plot. James took an active part in the trial of the accused, but he also claimed that the wildness of the storm came from the wild parts of Lapland and Finland, correlating witches with the wildness of wind and ocean. Mermaids were also believed to be able to cause storm and shipwreck.

All of this really indicates that magical fear rushes to fill a scientific vacuum; in the seventeenth century, people had no idea what caused wind. All they knew was that they were at its mercy, and they personified their fear in the figure of the witch.

OMEN READING

Really a tale as old as time: *every* culture has a form of omen reading. The ancient world saw the fall of every sparrow as an opportunity to prophesy. An eclipse of the moon led the Athenian army fatally to postpone their evacuation from Syracuse. When Alexander the Great was besieging the city of Tyre, many Tyrians dreamt that Apollo, who had a statue in the city, was turning away towards Alexander. This omen was believed to signify that Tyre would fall to Alexander. The Tyrians "encircled his colossal figure with cords and nailed it down to its pedestal, calling him an 'Alexandrist'." Alexander's own death was heralded by an exceptional number of omens: ravens falling dead at his feet as he approached Babylon, the city where he would indeed die; an animal sacrifice with a liver that had no lobe; a lion in his menagerie attacked and then killed by a tame ass; and a prisoner, wearing the royal diadem and robes, seated on Alexander's throne. After Alexander had died, everybody thought they had seen it coming, whether or not they truly had. The historian Thucydides describes omens before the Athenian expedition to Sicily, which ended in disaster.

On the eve of the Norman invasion of 1066, a comet arrived in the night sky, nearly as bright as the moon. Harold, the King of England, saw it as a very bad omen, while on the other side of the channel, William saw the same comet as a good omen and a message from God to press on with his attack. They were both right: William won the battle. The comet we now know to be Halley's Comet appears on the famous Bayeux Tapestry, the 70 m/230 ft long embroidery that depicts the events leading to the invasion of England and the Battle of Hastings.

If the gods failed to provide omens on this scale, seers might embark on active investigations. In the ancient world, this typically involved examining the body of an animal sacrifice. All armies in the ancient world travelled with a seer or mantis, and obviously, these were often wrong – but any errors could be explained away as misinterpretation, since omen reading was complex and intersectional.

CERIDWEN

Dearly loved by modern pagans, and at least partially invented by them in the form most familiar and to readers of fantasy literature, she came to represent a particularly Victorian idea of Celtic myth, fraught with Christian ideas of goodness. The Victorian poet Thomas Love Peacock (1785–1866) also wrote a poem, "The Cauldron of Ceridwen", rich in Gothic imagining.

The story comes from the *Tale of Taliesin*, which can be dated to around 1550. It concerns the hideous son of Ceridwen, a boy named Morvan – which means *cormorant* (his other possible name means *absolute darkness*). She decides to brew a cauldron of knowledge for him so that he will be exceptionally wise. Only the first three drops of the potion will contain the magic essence of knowledge. To make the potion, she consults the books of the *fferyllt*, a word deriving from the Welsh name for the Roman poet Virgil, who was believed to be a magician. Ceridwen sets a little boy called Gwion Bach to stoke the fire, telling him never to taste the brew. But while she sleeps, three drops spring from the cauldron, and Gwion pushes Morvan out of the way so he can get them. He runs away immediately, because with his newfound wisdom he knows she will be furious. After a lot of magical shape-shifting, she swallows him while she is in the form of a hen and he a grain. Nine months later she gives birth to a baby boy who is so beautiful that she cannot bring herself to kill him. Instead, she sets him adrift in a boat. The man who finds the boy names him Taliesin.

This is not really a female-centred myth at all, since it is all about Taliesin, rather than Ceridwen; whose significance is reduced to being the mother of a famous man. When compared with, say, the stories of Diana and Freyja, it seems less resonant, and much more in keeping with the Victorian ideology that popularized it.

BLACK MAGICK

As always, the *Oxford English Dictionary* has a simple formulation – "Magic involving the invocation of evil spirits; harmful or malevolent magic" – and it offers an illustrative quotation from 1635: "Some diuide this abstruse Art into Theurgia, White Magicke, and Goetia, Blacke Magicke, or the Blacke Art, otherwise called Necromantia", which comes from the hack writer and jobbing dramatist Thomas Heywood. Others say that black magic is anything performed with the assistance of the devil. This might be an interesting claim to make – see the documentary *Hail Satan?* (2019), which illustrates the mischievous but hardly evil use of Satanism solely for the purpose of opposing the Christian right.

Indeed, another way of describing *black magic* is as a lazy way of talking about magic that scares people. There's no doubt that the horror film industry has a lot to answer for in this respect. Furthermore, the term *black magic* has played an unpleasant role in the evolution of ideas about race that are based on skin colour.

Art historian Madeline Caviness has suggested that Christian Europeans began seeing themselves as white sometime in the middle of the thirteenth century. Up to that point, she suggests, flesh tones in medieval art depicted a range of pale colours, but from the middle of the thirteenth century onwards, whiteness became the colour of Christian European identity. From the late twelfth century through the thirteenth and onwards, Black Saharan Africans are depicted as the killers of John the Baptist or the torturers of Christ. Not long after that, and not insignificantly, the colour of Satan himself changes from blue to black. The earliest known suggested depiction of Satan is in a sixth-century mosaic, in the Basilica of Sant'Apollinare Nuovo, Ravenna, Italy, showing the devil as an ethereal blue angel. By the first half of the fourteenth century, when the illustrated manuscript known as The Smithfield Decretals (a copy of the *Decretals* of Gregory IX) was created, the devil is shown with talons, wings and a tail, being cast out by angels. And he is black.

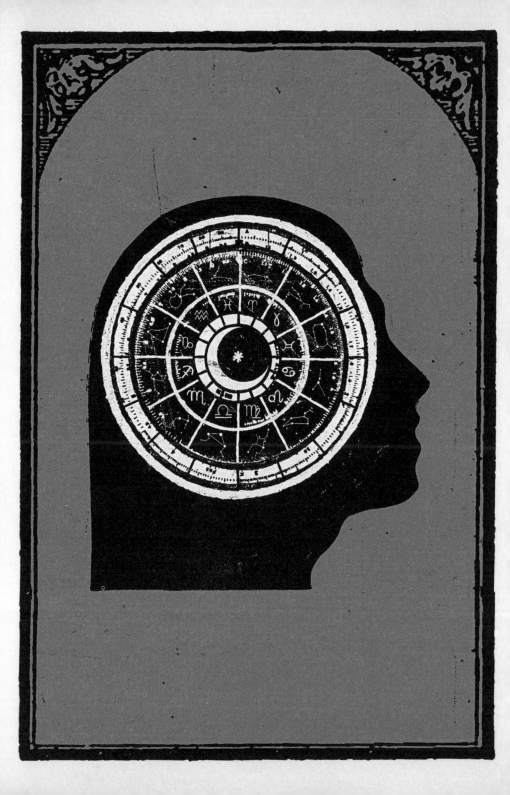

BIRTH CHART

This is a snapshot of the heavens at the exact moment when a person was born, showing the position of all planets and heavenly bodies, and the celestial zodiac signs they are occupying. Astrology is extremely complex, but the basic principle is that the planet, sign and house govern, determine or influence a particular area of life. For example, the moon is about emotions and the inner world.

Witchily, a birth chart is read counterclockwise, or widdershins. So we start with the ascendant (or rising) sign, the sign that is coming up on the horizon at the moment of birth. Some astrologers believe this is at least as significant as the sun sign, because it determines the way others see you. This can be absolutely different to your sun sign, which is what people normally mean when they say they are Cancer, or Scorpio.

How much does your birth chart matter? More importantly, how can you work with it as a magic user? The short answer is that the birth chart can tell us something about who we are, and, more importantly, what magical powers were born in us. That isn't the end of the story, but self-knowledge includes knowing and embracing our beginnings. In the same way that most of us now know that the time when Mercury is retrograde is not the ideal time to sign an important legal document, so we can work with our own magical planets and constellations. If we know that we face a year when Neptune is transiting in strong sextile with Saturn, we can be aware that changes are in store, and we can accept the need to embrace some of those changes for us. Much of witchcraft is acceptance of our true selves, rather than tinkering for conformity.

POTION

A magical medicine. *Potion* just means something you drink, so they are always liquid. Some words carry an extra witchy resonance. If I prepare a potion, I am doing something exciting and magical. If I prepare a bowl of chicken soup, I'm not. So what makes the difference? It isn't my attitude, because I could be making chicken soup infused with love and warmth. I could be drawing on the power of the chicken itself, power from its very bones, to treat and help the misery of a snuffly cold. Perhaps chicken soup is a potion, a healing spell; don't sell it short. However, and in general, when people talk about potions, they usually mean something that contains ingredients associated with the Otherworld.

A potion can also be called a *philtre* when its purpose is to induce love. This should never be confused with an aphrodisiac on the one hand, or a date rape drug on the other. There have been some dangerous materials in circulation as aphrodisiacs, including cantharides, or Spanish fly. To avoid all that, regard a potion as something to be infused with power and energy. Clear water is the best starting point.

As with amulets, names and images can be pertinent in potions too, and a common practice is to write a charm on rice paper, then dissolve it in a liquid to make a potion. You might write, "Give me your heart, as you have my heart" for a love potion, for example, or you might use a magic pentacle, ordinarily something you might physically place beneath the pillow of your beloved. Here is an ancient charm that has been used: *Sancitan Sanamiel Samafoelis*. If you don't know what it means, all the better.

There are also healing potions, some of which are simply herbal remedies, while others are infused with magical energy. For example, woundwort – yarrow, or *Achillea* – might stop bleeding, but it might be accompanied by a rite to increase its magical effect and strengthen the person to whom it is applied. Almost all such rites are invocations of higher powers. You can invoke any higher power in whose strength you believe – throughout the Middle Ages, the Virgin Mary was invoked most often of all. But you might simply say: "White horse, white horse, bring me good luck" or "Dock in, nettle out" – an invocation so old that it is used in Chaucer. Don't be afraid to insert your own words.

CANDLES

Much of witchcraft is about light and darkness. The great solar wheel of the year plunges us into the dark for what can seem like months on end; we are deprived of brightness. It's a fasting time, when some of us long for the return of light. When we sense the wheel beginning to turn, we choose to celebrate our hope for brighter days in a feast called Imbolc; the Christian term is Candlemas, and the story it tells is of a woman going out to meet the world for the first time after the imposed isolation of childbirth and care for a very small infant. This story is told about the Virgin Mary, but it also represents a profound experience for many women, an experience of darkness and isolation followed by bursting into light and celebrating reconnection.

From all of this, we derive two magical customs: the first is lighting a candle as a form of self-care (and particularly, lighting one rather than cursing the darkness, focusing our attention on the bright flame). The second is the Catholic ritual of lighting a candle as a prayer for somebody else. Another example of the kind of action often criticized by Protestants as magical, lighting a candle for somebody else expresses a hope and a longing to bring light back to their life. Sometimes, it's all we can do when we see somebody else in trouble, when we know that danger lies ahead for a person we love. It expresses faith that just as the sun returns, so other good things will return.

Much magic is about very small actions, tiny domestic deeds, and yet witchcraft above all understands – and has always understood – that such small domestic acts can tilt the whole world. Every time we light a candle, we celebrate life itself, the brief candle of our mortal existence.

I SHALL GO INTO A HARE,
WITH SORROW AND SYCH AND MEICKLE CARE;
AND I SHALL GO IN THE DEVIL'S NAME,
AY WHILE I COME HOME AGAIN.

To change back, she would say:

HARE, HARE, GOD SEND THEE CARE.
I AM IN A HARE'S LIKENESS NOW,
BUT I SHALL BE IN A WOMAN'S LIKENESS EVEN NOW.

HARE

Centuries before witches were associated with cats, they were linked to hares. Often visible in ploughed fields, hares are surprisingly swift, and they don't run straight but zigzag. Like most animals associated with witches, they are believed to be unlucky in folklore – or lucky, and it may be that the lucky rabbit's foot was originally the foot of a hare. The hare is another animal associated with the Otherworld; they have no home in this world, and like fairies are believed to come and go from elsewhere.

In ancient Greece and Rome, the hare was believed to be capable of changing sex, and hermaphroditic as well. Hares were therefore associated with same-sex love. Their queerness is part of what links them with the power of the witch, who is often neither male nor female, but both. Diana/Artemis (see page 206), goddess of wild places and the hunt, was also linked to hares, and newborn hares were not to be killed but left to her protection. The German goddess Holda was followed by a procession of hares bearing torches.

The Celtic goddess Ēostre could take the shape of a hare at each full moon; given that she lends her name to Easter, some folklorists connect this with the Easter Bunny. Witches could turn into hares, and they did so by possessing the body of a hare. To turn into a hare, Isobel Gowdie, the Scottish woman who confessed to witchcraft in 1662, said that she chanted the words opposite.

Isobel made her confession along with a series of statements about her visits to the land of the fairies – a fascinating insight into the connection between magical animals and magical beings.

I AND PANGUR BÁN MY CAT,
'TIS A LIKE TASK WE ARE AT:
HUNTING MICE IS HIS DELIGHT,
HUNTING WORDS I SIT ALL NIGHT.

CAT

Everybody knows that cats are magical. A black cat crossing a street in front of him terrified the witch-hunter Matthew Hopkins so much that he launched a witchcraft persecution to ensure his safety. For one thing, cats are like witches: ultimately solitary, giving their allegiance only to those deemed worthy. Unlike witches, they are confidently certain that they rule the world. And therefore, they are disobedient, not fully domesticated or tamed, a touch of the wild on the hearth. Because cats were allowed in monasteries, a beautiful Irish poem from the ninth century celebrates the similarities between catching rodents and catching thoughts in the words opposite.

The ancient Egyptians celebrated cats in the form of the goddess Bast. As Terry Pratchett said, cats have never forgotten that they were once worshipped. Bast is not unrelated to Sekhmet, the lioness goddess who represents the power of the desert, its heat and strength and energy, power that could be harnessed against enemies in times of war. Cats were also associated with the goddess Diana, the virgin mistress of wild nature (see page 206). The sense that cats have a secret life of their own unseen by human beings is celebrated in the folktale about the king of the cats, told as early as 1553. In the story, a traveller hears a cat say, "Tell Tom Tildrum that Tybbal is dead." The man repeats the words at an inn, and immediately the housecat cries: "Then I am the king of the cats!", rushes up the chimney, and is never seen again.

A black cat called Sathan was regarded as important evidence of malevolent witchcraft in one of the first large-scale English witch trials, the 1566 Essex trial. Despite their usefulness as hunters of rodents, cats were also seen as unruly because they had a secret life not subject to human governance. The Dominicans sought cats as being especially likely to work with witches; by contrast, dogs could be relied upon to bark ferociously at heretics. Robert Darnton gives a horrifying account of what he calls the Great Cat Massacre in the late 1730s in Paris, where half-dead cats were tried and found guilty of witchcraft, and strung up. The demonization of cats illustrates the unpopularity of aloofness and steely resolve.

CURSE

It used to be said by modern pagans that cursing and hexing were a bad idea because whatever is sent out returns threefold (some even say tenfold). (*Hex* derives from the word *Hexe*, or *Häxe*, the words for witch in German and Swedish.) However, this idea is really recent and probably influenced by Christianity.

In the ancient and medieval worlds, cursing was common. It was one of the most common charges against witches. However, the term *curse* is confusing, because it can sometimes simply mean speaking abusively to a person, rather than a supernatural action that invokes and brings down bad luck or harm. However, both involve words, whether written down or said out loud. Virtually all cultures have curses, and Mesopotamian and Egyptian cultures used a wide variety, as did the Greeks and Romans, often writing their ill wishes on cursed tablets. Examples survive, and they are typically dismaying in their violence. Curses can include condemning an enemy to childlessness, to insomnia until death, to bad luck in a variety of undertakings, to shipwreck and storms, to nightmares, and to being unable to have sex except with the person performing the curse. Typically, in the ancient world, curses involved invoking the aid of a deity. Usually, this would be a deity specific to the area of activity covered by the curse. Sometimes, the material parts of animals were used, or an animal sacrifice might be included in the right. Love charms could actually be more frightening than direct curses since these usually involved an element of compulsion.

Curses were often aimed at rectifying a wrong; people might for example curse somebody who had stolen an item from them, as this Roman example shows: "The human who stole Verio's cloak or his things, who deprived him of his property, may he be bereft of his mind and memory, be it a woman or those who deprived Verio of his property, may the worms, cancer, and maggots penetrate his hands, head, feet, as well as his limbs and marrows." Note that this curse carries on working even after death.

Curses may also attach themselves to objects, whether the Hope diamond or the tomb of Tutankhamun.

PREGNANT BODY

Witchcraft is all about transformation, and the power to transform and change ourselves. Pregnancy is a direct and incredibly powerful experience of bodily change – and the word *incredibly* is a fair one. It is amazing that a body can change so much in a relatively short time, and can grow another body inside itself. A pregnant body is miraculous – and also monstrous.

It is therefore not surprising that the pregnant body was credited both with magical power, and also with exceptional vulnerability to the magical powers of others. The pregnant body was almost considered contagious, and a lot of folklore is connected with it. For example, sitting in a chair after a pregnant woman was supposed to lead immediately to pregnancy yourself. Parsley was believed to cause pregnancy or, in some traditions, to lead to abortion, and similar tales are told about lettuce. Other and more disturbing kinds of folklore show that blemishes in a newborn baby were nearly always blamed on the mother. For example, the harelip was supposed to be caused by seeing a hare while pregnant, and strawberry marks was supposed to be caused by a craving for strawberries. In traditional societies, the pregnant woman was therefore seen as vulnerable, even to passing thoughts or passing animals, and many rituals were sought to protect from ill will.

In childbirth, the woman in labour was sequestered and only women were allowed to enter the birthing room, with even the known father of the child exiled until 10 days after the birth – which was also the first moment at which the new mother was allowed to sit up and bedsheets changed. All this was because unchristened and unnamed children, as well as unchurched women (after childbirth, women were supposed to attend a Christian church service to be cleansed), were seen as especially vulnerable to evil magic. Indeed, numerous witchcraft accusations were levelled against women called keepers, or lying-in maids, whose role was to look after both the new mother and her baby. It was easy for women in that position to appear to usurp the mother's role, and take magical control of her body and that of her child.

NECROMANCY

When the first generation of modern pagan witches burst out of the broom cupboard, they were understandably eager to distinguish themselves as sharply as possible from the lurid imagining of male witch-hunters. As a result, they worked hard to produce a very clean and un-disturbing version of paganism, which left out some of the principal sources of its magic and its magical thinking. Among aspects left on the cutting room floor were the use and reuse of the dead, both as continuing presences and as physical traces. However, many modern pagans might now concede that it has not been possible to produce a version of paganism anodyne enough to reassure its critics. It may therefore be time to admit that much of the magic of witches in every period has something to do with the dead. The presence of the dead is an easy way of answering the question of where magic comes from.

Necromancy, a compound of Ancient Greek νεκρός (*nekrós*, or "dead body") and μαντεία (*manteía*, or "divination"), is also the term for the practice of magical sorcery involving communication with the dead by summoning their spirits for the purpose of divination; imparting the means to foretell future events; and discovering hidden knowledge. Some modern practitioners might describe this as spiritualism because of the associations between necromancy and evil magic. However, it is the purpose of magic that may make it evil, not the means.

There is often some awareness that necromancy can be spelled as nigromancy (see Black Magick, page 136), reinforcing the association of witchcraft with what is hidden (occult) and secret. Like their classical predecessors, the witches in *Macbeth* use body parts for divination, and so too did many of the witches persecuted in the sixteenth and seventeenth centuries. As did Shakespeare's Prospero. One way of defining witches is to describe them as people who have a different relationship with the dead.

FAMILIAR

Do you have a pet? A small animal that follows you around, whether it's a cat or a dog? Are you absolutely sure that it is not a demon? Once, your neighbours would not have been at all certain, and would have been inclined to interpret even a persistent fly as a devil in your service.

The familiar demon, and in the shape of an animal, is peculiar to English witchcraft. In other places, animals associated with witchcraft and demons are very large and impressive (wolves, deer). What is peculiar about the English familiar is the apparent affection in which they are held. They are given pet names, like Tiffin or Robin, and while they may be fed by suckling the witch's blood, like very small vampires, it is also common for them to be fed on milk or cream. This may give us a clue about what they "really" were: the standard household spirit, often called the hob or the brownie, which might help with housework and animal husbandry in exchange for a bowl of cream, as long as it was never thanked and no attempt was ever made to give it clothing. Such creatures were understood to be capricious, and they were also covered in thick fur.

By the time of the witchcraft persecutions, Puritan thinking had ensured that complex categorizations of ambivalent beings had broken down, to be replaced by the idea that everything which was not God was a devil, so a witch being asked about domestic help might have given answers that her interrogators saw as a confession of demonic assistance when she had only been describing the brownie.

But even the greatest in the land were not spared from this kind of suspicion. During the English Civil War, the Royalist general Prince Rupert took his large poodle dog Boy into battle with him. Throughout the war the dog was greatly feared among the Parliamentarian forces and credited with supernatural powers to protect Rupert and himself. The dog was killed at the battle of Marston Moor, and the Parliamentarians were very glad to see it gone.

SEASONS OF THE WITCH

Like the phases of the moon and the Zodiac year, the seasons all have specific witchy associations of their own.

Many modern pagans follow a reconstructed "Celtic" calendar from winter solstice to winter solstice, but in the past that calendar was inflected by the intersectional Christian year, which was itself strongly tied to nature and landscape. Specific markers, often called quarter days, came to characterize likely moments of a thinning veil between the worlds. The most famous of these in the modern world is Halloween, or Samhain (pronounced So-win). There are others, however – including Walpurgisnacht, called Beltane in the "Celtic" calendar, which takes place on April 30, the eve of May Day.

The dates that assume a special significance for Scottish witches come from the Christian calendar – in a way. The first is Holy Cross Day, or Holy Rood Day, September 14. This is the day from which Holyrood Palace gets its name. It was also associated with nutting, going into the countryside to gather nuts, and nuts can be magical, especially hazelnuts (see Tree, page 98). Moreover, the vision that leads to the feast day has strong pagan overtones. The Church might think that it is about St Helena's discovery of the True Cross (though ask anyone Welsh about Helen of the Roads), but the local legend is about a king who goes hunting in the wild and is assailed by a white stag of gigantic size, which had been maddened by the pursuit, "noise and din of bugles". Going hunting is a common time for encountering another world (see also Deer, Hare , pages 54 and 144). The Christian version here means that David I of Scotland sees a silver cloud, from which a hand emerges to give the king a sparkling cross of miraculous construction, insofar that the material of which it was composed could never be discovered. Unsurprisingly, given the magical associations of deer, Holy Cross Day sees people emerging into the countryside as King David did, also encountering otherworldly signs, notably magical stags. Whenever times are borderline or liminal, magic enters in.

PENTACLE

When a circle is drawn around the five-pointed star (or Pentagram), it becomes a Pentacle. Obviously, this connects with the meaning of the number 5, which can include gender queerness. It is a synthesis of complementary powers, the masculine and the feminine, and body integrated with spirit.

A circle has no beginning and no ending. So too the geometric form called the endless knot. Beginnings and endings can serve as points of entry, and these endless forms are therefore more secure and better at safeguarding the magic user and their space (see Witch Marks, pages 30 and 32). The word *abracadabra* has the same structure, with no beginning and no end, and no intrinsic meaning.

The pentacle is ancient. The Pythagoreans used the pentacle in the way that Christians were to use the cross, as a welcome symbol and an identification badge. In Christian times, it becomes a symbol of the five senses, and appears on the shield of Sir Gawain in the poem *Gawain and the Green Knight*. Another illustration of the magic of five objects was the banner of the five wounds of Jesus Christ, used in the enormous rebellion called the Pilgrimage of Grace. For Cornelius Agrippa, the polymath and occult writer, the five points of the star represented the five elements (earth, fire, air, water and ether), so that it encompassed the entire world. Not until the nineteenth century does the idea develop that a reversed pentacle or pentagram is a symbol of evil or Satanism: it was interpreted as overturning the proper order of things, and representing the triumph of matter over spirit. The two points of the star facing upwards were interpreted as the horns of a goat or the horns of Satan. Despite its prevalence in secular horror films, this interpretation is not ancient at all, but is part of a Romantic misreading of an ancient symbol.

MORTARS AND PESTLES

The mortar is the sturdy circular bowl, typically made of stone or pottery, and sometimes made of metal; the pestle is the blunt, clublike implement that crushes and changes.

Again we move into the kitchen, into the domestic, but also back into the past. The mortar and pestle is the last surviving trace of one of the oldest domestic implements, the quern. A circle with a hole, and a long implement to penetrate it; the symbology is not subtle. In a way, the mortar and pestle offer a crude image of how sex and reproduction work, and offer the changed substance as a birth. When we think about grinding grain, we also think about transforming and metamorphosing the wild; we should also think about rhythm, and about the work of women as gatherers and transformers. When you use a mortar and pestle to grind herbs or spices, you are performing an action that unites you with the women of the past. This can be the subject of reflection; rather than seeing grinding to powder as a dreary manual task, it offers the opportunity to engage fully not only with the material substance used in magic, but also with past magic users. Traditionally, many magical spells involve fine powders.

And in case you are wondering why a mortar and pestle is connected with witchcraft, consider Baba Yaga. This Slavic witch figure flies in a mortar, using a pestle to push herself along. Like the mortar and pestle, she is both helpful and terrifying in her power. When Vasilisa the Wise visits her, Vasilisa receives benefits and help, including the transformative power of the skull lamp, which symbolizes the witch ability to manage death, but Baba Yaga also murders Vasilisa's entire family. She is impossible to sum up: she is Cloud, Moon, Death, Winter, Snake, Bird, Pelican or Earth Goddess, totemic matriarchal ancestress, female initiator, phallic mother. Above all, she is a hag with affinities to Perchta and Holda, and she represents the power to crush and to transform. A kitchen tool is once again an element in the power of the witch.

THESSALIAN WHEEL

Also called a whirligig, which sounds like the name for a children's toy, this is in fact a powerful magical device from the ancient world, which can be used to draw down the moon, to pull crops or milk from one place to another, and to draw a lover to the house of the witch who loves them. The whirligig is especially associated with Hekate – and has also been used for weather magic, to draw rain down from the sky. It is also linked with the Moirai, the Fates, who wove the threads of each person's life.

Mythology supplied an explanation for the device and its power, through the tale of a woman called Lynx who used such a wheel to enchant Zeus, king of the gods. Zeus's wife, Hera, transformed Lynx into a bird, a specific type of bird called the wryneck, or jinx. In English, a jinx is a kind of curse, which can be brought about by two people saying a word at the same moment, or by overpraising something or speaking as if success was a certainty. How does this relate to the idea of a wheel? Perhaps what goes around comes around... And perhaps there is something extraordinary about a wheel; it can make heavy loads move smoothly along, can pull thread and rope. When the power to attract is imagined, it takes that shape.

In a poem by Theocritus, from the fourth century BCE, a girl steals down to the crossroads to perform a magical spell, to restore her lover Delphis's passion for her. She works her magic using the wheel, and the refrain: *Turn, magic wheel, and pull that man after me.* It's hypnotic, incantatory. She also performs a fire spell, burning herbs and flowers, bread and grain. "Where are my bay-leaves? Come, Thestylis; where are my love-charms? Come crown me the bowl with the crimson flower o' wool." She sends her maid with the ashes of her offering to place on the lintel of Delphis's doorway, and while she waits, she tells the story of their relationship to the listening moon. She is assisted by Hekate, but we never see if the magic works.

COMPASS

Many world religions orient prayer by the points of the compass, and modern paganism is no exception. While the religions of the book have a preferred direction – east – pagans see each direction as productive in its own way.

It's possible to use a compass to determine direction, but it's also possible and, arguably, preferable to determine direction by noticing where the sun comes up, and where it goes down, and the fall of light, or the stars in the sky, especially the North Star or the Southern Cross.

While north is sometimes seen in negative terms by Christians, its cold power, focus and strength can be critical to magic. The south is the opposite – fire, heat – and an image such as a circle or pentacle can balance these two capacities. East represents awakening, and the bright powers of new ideas and a mental refresh. West represents the turbulent beauty of the ocean, and the complex feelings it symbolizes.

Unlike Western science, witchcraft always seeks to incorporate all of the human, rather than creating a hierarchy where one direction is good and the others are bad. In the same way, witchcraft wants to notice both ideas and feelings, bodies and minds. This is not just a question of balance, of giving equal weight to all the different parts of ourselves; it's also a question of orienting ourselves many times towards what we are thinking and feeling from moment to moment, accepting differences within ourselves. Do I contradict myself? Very well then, I contradict myself; I am large, I contain multitudes. Like music and poetry, witchcraft embraces ambivalence rather than trying to resolve it hastily. The degrees of the compass (all 360) are for us and with us.

AVALON

If witches have a homeland for which we yearn, it's Avalon. It's part of being a witch to be perpetually an outsider, but Avalon is the place where we can dream of belonging. We don't have to accept the wonky history sometimes offered by others to understand what Avalon is, and we certainly don't have to buy into some of the rather toxic myths of racial identity that accompany it. However, it is close to the gates of the underworld, and as such it connects us with the past, and with the dead.

The story of Avalon begins in the eleventh century, with Geoffrey of Monmouth, who names "Avallo" as the place where Arthur's sword Excalibur is made, and where he goes to be healed of his wounds by his half-sister Morgan. It is an island in a lake, and many attempts have been made to locate it. It has often been identified with Glastonbury, and particularly with Glastonbury Tor, but all sorts of other places have also been suggested. Rather than thinking of Avalon as a physical place, we might think of it as a place we can make for ourselves, a place to recharge, to recreate energy and move back into the world refreshed. In that sense, everybody needs their own Avalon.

Here is how to make one in your mind. You are lying on your back, on green grass, under a blossoming apple tree. The sky over your head is a deep blue. The scent of the flowers reaches you, with a soft breeze from the nearby lake. The earth beneath you holds and supports you. You feel its immensity recharge you. Slowly, your taut muscles relax. If your mind begins to give way to the use of half sleep, you realize that many others have lain the way you are now, under this same tree, awaiting the moment when they can be healed enough to go back into the world. Their strength too is now yours. Your journey has been a journey into their story, and now you can carry back their magic into the world.

POPPETS

Poppets have joined clowns in the ranks of things that were once considered cute but are now seen as scary. There's a reason for that. Historically, witches sometimes used wax models of other people to harm or cure, mostly the former. One group of witches at Windsor made a wax dummy of Elizabeth I and stuck pins in it in an attempt at assassination. Like much magic, it works on the basis of reproduction, and the principle *As above, so below*: what happens in a very small space, such as the kitchen, can affect what happens in a much larger space, such as a whole country.

But it's not just the idea of being harmed at a distance that's scary. Behind the poppet lies the uncomfortable idea of the doppelgänger. In Scotland, this being is called a *fetch*. A sighting of a fetch is generally taken as a portent of its double's looming death. But the idea of meeting a double is troubling anyway, because we all believe in our own uniqueness.

As Naomi Klein recently said, "the person we think we are is fundamentally vulnerable to forces outside of our control." These forces may be inside ourselves as well as outside. The witchy ability to see outside ourselves, or to see our own bodies at a distance, is alarming and disconcerting. There is a psychiatric disorder called Capgras syndrome in which someone comes to believe that a friend, spouse, parent, close family member or pet has been replaced by an identical impostor. Shivery. And in the age of artificial intelligence, many of us are especially aware of the risks of duplication, of being cloned on social media, of having our identities usurped or traduced. In the twenty-first century, all of us have a digitized poppet which can be stabbed to the heart.

What to do? Traditionally, seeing a doppelgänger or finding out about a poppet means the need to go on a journey; what insights are being offered, and can they be taken in or extruded? Seeing ourselves from the outside is an opportunity for healing as well as harm.

HOODOO

This is the spiritual or magical practice established among African-American communities, incorporating elements from African and white religious and folk-healing traditions; some anthropologists have suggested that hoodoo is African religion hybridized with European Protestant Christianity, while voodoo is African religion hybridized with European Catholic Christianity. The issue is complicated by the fact that *hoodoo* has also been used as a general word for a magical curse, and is also used negatively with racist connotations.

Foot track magic is a hoodoo practice that involves cursing someone by a wide variety of methods, such as placing stones in a certain configuration in the person's path, sprinkling goofer dust (the word *goofer* comes from the Kikongo word *kufwa*, meaning *to die*) or graveyard dirt in their shoes, or placing dirt from their footprint into a bottle. Some of the sharpest references to hoodoo survive in African-American music, such as Ma Rainey's 'Black Dust Blues':

> *Lord, I was out one morning, found black dust all round my door*
> *I began to get thin, had trouble with my feet*
> *Throwing dust about the house whenever I tried to eat*
> *Black dust in my window, black dust on my porch mat*
> *Black dust's got me walking on all fours like a cat.*

Hoodoo practices were common enough in Mississippi in the 1920s and 1930s that Delta blues artists like Robert Johnson made use of them in 'Stones in My Passway':

> *Now you tryin' to take my life, and all my lovin' too*
> *You laid a passway for me, now what are you tryin' to do?*

A hoodoo curse can range from giving the hoodooed person bad luck or memory loss to causing incurable disease and death. What is fantastic about this is its unapologetic ferocity. Anyone used to the milk and water versions of Dianic witchcraft might well be surprised. But this is magic replete with the anger of a people enslaved, and later marginalized and oppressed. All of us can learn from it. Witchcraft has to be about anger and our sense of justice, not just about being calm and kind.

GRIMOIRE

A book of magic. Obviously, all books are magic, in that they carry us away into another world, but a grimoire is specifically a book of spells.

Posh, expensive magic always made use of books. John Dee's *Monas Hieroglyphi*a (1564) draws on what was interpreted as the oldest book of magic, the fourth-century book *Hermetica*, featuring the work associated with Hermes Trismegistus, including astrology, and others alchemy, while another compilation of texts, the *Kyranides*, offers healing spells and remedies. The two most important examples of bookish magic are the *Key of Solomon* and the *Sworn Book of Honorius*, medieval magical texts that offer a process of elaborate spiritual training to enable the magic user eventually to converse with angelic powers that will do their bidding. Then we have Cornelius Agrippa's books of occult philosophy, and, amusingly, Reginald Scot's book *The Discoverie of Witchcraft* (1584), in which Scot sceptically writes down a number of spells, enabling them to be reused by aspirant magicians.

Other grimoires include the eighteenth-century *Petit Albert* (*Lesser Albert*) and the *Grand Grimoire*, also known as *Le Dragon Rouge* (*The Red Dragon*), still in use in the Caribbean, and notoriously containing an invocation to Satan himself (see Black Magick, page 136).

Most people who practised witchcraft, however, did not learn about it from books but from oral tradition, which was also how most handicrafts and manual skills were learned. Many families kept a small manuscript book of spells and remedies, including both medical and magical, sometimes on the same page, and many also included alchemical methods. This kind of grimoire was highly personal, and often organized around the kinds of needs that its creator might experience in a normal week. The very many cunning women who were arrested as witches were often part of this tradition. Such magic was secret because it was commercially viable. One such surviving charm, folded repeatedly and sealed with wax, also contained a powerful curse on any man or woman who touches the property of named individuals. Augmented with cabalistic signs, such written charms could be sewn into clothing or placed to guard property. The simplest and most common such magic was the word *abracadabra*.

POSTMENOPAUSAL BODY

In pictures of witches from the age of witch persecution, one feature stands out: most witches are old. They have postmenopausal bodies – sagging breasts, bulging tummies, skinny thighs, wrinkled faces. It's not too much to say that the image of the wicked witch as old and therefore ugly is one of the most powerful pieces of marketing in history. Nobody wants to look like a wicked witch. Everybody, therefore, is willing to buy products to ensure that they do not resemble such a fearsome being. Of course, there are many other, better ways to pamper yourself, but a lot of advertising is based on the idea that there is something wrong with you which needs a product to fix.

But why are postmenopausal women objects of disgust? The answer is the construction of the female body in a male-dominated world where heterosexuality is the only thing regarded as normal. We are constantly told that we simply have to reproduce, because that is what we are; that is *all* we are. For us to be attractive, we have to seem childlike and powerless. There is immense power available in seeing this trap, and in taking back the body – past, present and future – from this poisonous ideology.

Where there is fear, there is power. The magic of embracing the postmenopausal body, seeing its beauty, treating it generously and lovingly, is a potent magic, a queer magic, and it is scary. It is especially scary if witches start altering their idea of beauty away from the one imposed on us, and towards the one we ourselves feel. When do we have the most wrinkles in our faces? When we smile, when we laugh.

Nothing divides older and younger women so much as the demand that older women look like younger women, and that younger women prevent themselves from looking like older ones. In the witch trials, younger women are often the first to accuse older women who have exploited them. If that period teaches us anything, it is that we must hang together, or we will surely hang separately. Women of all ages need to embrace the queer hag for strength.

HEKATE

We think we know her. The goddess of witches and magic, midnight, crossroads; the old crone of the dark moon.

But she was none of these things until late in the fifth century BCE. It was only then that she became the teacher of magic and witches, perhaps because of a tragedy in which the violent, abandoned witch Medea calls on her. She who inhabited the inmost reaches of the house, the dark safe places, now became the goddess of poison and ghosts, of revenge and the darkest of magics. She was worshipped in liminal places, outside the city gates, where she drank unmixed wine and ate red mullet – otherwise taboo because it was considered polluted – as well as dog meat and special cakes. She was accompanied by packs of barking hell hounds and hosts of ghostlike revenants, and she protected wounds and crossroads, and the gates of Hades. She can make any magic spell more powerful.

But before that, she was a helper. She helps Demeter to find her lost daughter Persephone in the underworld, when Persephone has been abducted (see page 74). In this role, she had a part to play in the Eleusinian mysteries of Demeter. She could join with Artemis/Diana as a goddess of childbirth, protecting the unborn baby. She may have been identified with the Babylonian goddesses of the underworld, Ereshkigal, which might explain her links to the quest to find Persephone. This goes with the fact that Hesiod praises her as a powerful goddess of the earth, sea and sky, who protects warriors and fishermen.

Her name is pronounced *He-cart-ay* and she is invoked as Lady Hekate of the heavens, Hekate of the underworld, Hekate of the three roads, Hekate of the triple face, Hekate of the single phase. She is chthonic, a goddess of the realms below, deep in the earth, where the dead keep their secrets. Yet it is from there that new plant life springs, and that is why she is the one who *keeps in mind the vigour of nature*. She knows the deeps.

BREASTS

There are few things witchier or queerer than breasts understood not as secondary sexual characteristics but as food sources. Louise Bourgeois's *Good Mother* sculpture of a nursing woman encased in a bell jar illustrates our wish to turn a mother into an inorganic function. To this day, breastfeeding in public is often controversial, attracting many complaints, in part because baring a breast is interpreted as sexual, and in part because touching a breast is also seen that way. In general, society does not like being reminded that breasts exist not to gratify desire but to provide milk. It seems especially confusing within Western culture that a woman can be at one and the same time a mother and a sexual being. As with transphobia and fear of the postmenopausal body, the prejudice against breastfeeding women illustrates perfectly the supposed function of the breast in culture – that is, as a fetish.

In taking back the breast, and using it as they please, women have been accused of positive perversity (see Familiar, page 154 and Witch Marks, pages 30 and 32). Lady Macbeth, in her invocation to the powers of darkness, begs them to "take my milk for gall", depriving her breasts of the power to nourish anything but a demon.

The fact is that breastfeeding doesn't seem natural in a world where few of us have seen anybody do it before being abruptly called to do it ourselves. It is a physical skill, a learned physical skill, and surprisingly complex, with the result that many women despite their best efforts find they can't do it. This can be a desperate struggle between a mother and a new baby, who is literally tearing the skin of her breasts due to an imperfect latch. It looks like the kind of thing black magic might create when a baby comes off the breast with a mouthful of milk and blood mixed. Cunning women, local magic users in pre-industrial Europe, sometimes accused of malevolent witchcraft, may have tried to help women with breastfeeding, but in the period before antibiotics, mastitis and breast abscesses increased the risk and pain, and probably also the perception of risk and pain.

STATUES

A statue is erected to honour somebody or something. Some time ago, Marina Warner demonstrated that abstract qualities like peace and justice are usually personified as female figures, as are nation states (Britannia, and France's Marianne). We might want to find in such representations a trace of the real power of living women, but in fact it often seems to work the opposite way: a female figure of justice does not guarantee that women will be taken seriously as judges or lawyers. The risk is that we will be deceived by such female representation into believing that things are more equal than they are.

Witches know better. It takes more than placing a goddess statue on an altar to overthrow established powers. Nevertheless, it's a start. In magic, a statue plays a role similar to that of a poppet or a talisman; it's a focal point. As a focal point, it needs to affirm as well as instruct – many statues of women in every period are governed by toxic bodily norms and equally toxic gender ideologies. As Nietzsche says, when you stare into an abyss, you become an abyss; look carefully, and look sceptically.

Seek out the transgressive. Santa Muerte, the Bony Lady of Mexico, brings together an ancient Aztec goddess and a Catholic reminder of death; she likes offerings of hard liquor and cigarettes. Artemis of Ephesus, covered in breasts, is a monstrous maternity. Many goddess statues betray the heteronormative reproductive essentialism of some modern paganism, insisting that bodily maternity is the only way to be a mother. It ain't necessarily so. Witches know that maternity is emotional as well as physical, and in any case is physical for only a relatively short time – anyone can be a carrier of anybody who needs care. There are not, and there should not be, physiological rules to be a goddess. Within all of us lies the power to comfort, to sustain and to strengthen. Find a statue that makes that feel true for you.

ALTAR

The altar was not connected with witchcraft until the advent of modern paganism, which initially wanted to turn witchcraft into an organized religion. Therefore, various materials familiar from the religions of the book were imported into modern pagan practice, and their ancient origins stressed. However, the English Wiccan Gerald Gardner and his coven had no intention of reviving the uses of the altar in the ancient pagan world, because these largely involved animal sacrifice. In part, this was because Gardner was eager to avoid triggering the Satanist fantasies of his opponents, which also involved sacrifices on altars and Gothic notions of the black mass derived from the nineteenth-century French historian Jules Michelet.

Human sacrifice was not unknown in the ancient world, especially among particular cultures, including the Gauls and the Carthaginians. The city-state of ancient Carthage was a Phoenician colony located in what is now Tunisia; founded in around 800 BCE, it was destroyed by the Romans in 146 BCE. Children – both male and female, and mostly a few weeks old – were sacrificed by the Carthaginians at locations known as *tophets*. Dedications from the children's parents to the gods are inscribed on slabs of stone above their cremated remains, ending with the explanation that the god or gods concerned "had heard my voice and blessed me". In the Christian Bible, human sacrifices to pagan deities are described as devil worship, which led later Christians to decide that all such sacrifices were diabolical, and the baby-killing Carthaginians re-presented as witches.

In the ancient world, animal sacrifice – and possibly human sacrifice as well – was a dramatization of killing and violence and the guilt that goes with violence, like a Greek tragedy, and also a way of legitimating meat-eating by treating the taking of life that necessarily precedes it as a ritual, a licensed act. In the same way, the Gaulish practice of sacrificing prisoners of war can be part of a ritualization of killing. The problem with eliminating all such violence from our altars is that we then have no way of managing the complexity of violence in our lives, or our dealings with death and with our enemies.

EARTH AND GROUNDING

Earth is one of the four elements. However, it's often seen as the least magical, the one that cures magic, the one that's associated with an everyday world of practical business matters. Traditionally, high magic belittles a practical interest in money and business. Yet Earth has a special magic of its own. It's our home; it's where we begin, as the clay moulded by God, and it's where we end, in the dust of the grave.

Earth is considered to be passive; it is represented by the symbol for Taurus, and is referred to the lower left point of the pentagram in the Supreme Invoking Ritual of the Pentagram. To the syncretic magicians of the Golden Dawn, the elemental weapon of earth is the Pentacle. The archangel of earth is Uriel, and the earth elementals (following Paracelsus) are called gnomes, which is why it's appropriate to have them in gardens.

Many of these associations have since spread throughout the occult community. In astrology Taurus, Virgo or Capricorn: doers, makers, pragmatists. In tarot, Pentacles or Coins: good sense, and the pleasures of practicality. Yet crafts, and especially the crafts of pottery and metalsmithing, have long magical associations. Earth and those who can transform it are god-like in their powers.

It is seen as vital to ground and centre at the end of any magical ritual, to bring to a close any magical processes and to channel any excess energy out of our own bodies and into the ground. Obviously, the underlying metaphor is of electricity. Yet something else is also at work, something closer to witchcraft. The Earth is where people are ultimately buried; burying the person – laying them to rest – is an analogy for grounding in magic. It completes a circuit and ends a process.

RAVEN

Large, black, carrion-eating, and typically living on inimical landscapes of bare rock and mountain, ravens are powerful and therefore scary. Secular horror films present all corvids as in league with Satan. In Irish literature, ravens can sometimes be hopeful: they warn of the approach of enemies and help heroes in battle. That said, there are associations with two of the Irish goddesses (see page 36) that are seen as most uncomfortable and destructive, and frequently negatively portrayed in fantasy fiction. One is the Morrigan, who inspires battlefield prowess but also wears the bloodstained clothes of those fated to die; the other is Badb Catha, whose name means Battle Raven, and who confronts the armies of Ulster on the battlefield, warning of death and gloating over the corpses. (These goddesses may well be one and the same.) In a way, these goddesses are ravens. All this emphasizes the raven's link to death, which also explains their role as oracles.

An invented tale from the nineteenth century speaks of the ravens of the Tower of London; it is said that if the ravens ever leave, the Tower will fall. Though this legend is first recorded in the nineteenth century, it may have a basis in a much earlier story. In the Welsh *Mabinogion*, compiled in the twelfth and thirteenth centuries, King Brân the Blessed orders his followers to cut off his head and bury it beneath the White Hill, facing out towards France, as a talisman to protect Britain from foreign invasion. *Brân* is the modern Welsh word for raven, and the White Hill is where the White Tower (the keep of the Tower of London) now stands. The knowledge that Brân's head is buried beneath the White Hill would have served as protective reassurance in the Celtic tradition, just as modern ideas about the presence of ravens at the Tower does – but notice how the rewritten legend is a little bit defanged, turning a scary human body part into a story about pets.

OCEAN

Water is the witch's element, because like the witch, it gets into everything, has a part in everything, leaks and spills. It looks innocent, as if you could hold it in a fist, but it always escapes you. When gathered, water is one of the greatest powers on earth. The rapturous thunder of the breakers on the shore, foaming and creaming against the bare skin of the bather, is natural magic, a champagne given for nothing to everyone, and recent experiments in physics by a woman – of course – has revealed the importance of those bubbles in the workings of the great blue machine of ocean currents.

For the witch, the spectacle of the ocean reflects her own strengths and her connection with nature. Not for nothing is the word for *sea* feminine in many languages. Every woman who has defied convention to swim or sail or surf is a sea witch. Yet the association between witches and the sea has terrified men for centuries. Not least, James VI of Scotland, who came to believe that the witches of North Berwick had prevented his ship from reaching port, holding it static in a contrary wind while the witches themselves sailed joyfully around in sieves. Ridiculous though the story is, the grain of truth in it is important: the witches were intolerable because they were at home in nature. The sea witch in *The Little Mermaid* is portrayed as the epitome of devouring older femininity, and yet her power over the arcane dead of the sea is potent and even exciting, while the portrayal of the sea witch in the Disney film, based on the drag artist Divine, made positive the visibility of witchy femininity as a joyful masquerade.

The depths of the ocean are full of secrets, and secrets are powerful and terrifying. The ocean is the sister of the witch, and her symbol.

MENHIR

As a child, I tried every wardrobe door I came across. I was looking for the Otherwhere of Narnia. While Narnia's creator would have wanted me to understand this as a realization that I longed for heaven, it could equally well have been that I longed for magic and, above all, for magic that intersected with maps. Lewis may or may not have been wrong about heavenly longings, but probably right about my postcolonial situation; my ancestors had been dumped in Australia, and deracinated, with the results that they never felt at home in the landscape, scratching its surface while the First Nation Australians understood every pebble.

By contrast, the landscape of Europe is marked by forever culture. Among them are the great stones known as menhirs, which unite northern European cultures with African and Asian cultures. The word comes from Breton, and means *long stone*. A menhir is a large upright stone, emplaced in the ground by humans, typically dating from the European middle Bronze Age. They can be found individually as monoliths, or as part of a group of similar stones. Menhirs' size can vary considerably, but they often taper towards the top. There are about 50,000 surviving examples in the British Isles, including Ireland, and a further 12,000 in France. Yet we know almost nothing about the people who placed them, or about their original purpose. We have recently discovered that they are far older than was once believed; they may date from six or seven thousand years ago.

They mark something we can no longer see. Were they used by druids for human sacrifice? Were they territorial markers? Were they elements of a complex ideological system serving as mnemonic systems for oral cultures? Did they function as early calendars? Might they have been gateways to another world altogether, or markers of otherworldly presences? The enigmatic quality of these great stones does not detract from their magic, but rather enhances it.

CAVE

Another dark, womb-like space, mysterious and possibly connected to something even darker and more mysterious, namely the underworld, or hell itself.

Caves have long been associated with women and magic. In ancient Rome, the Sibyl was a mortal who attained longevity when Apollo offered to grant her a wish in exchange for her virginity. She took a handful of sand and asked for as many years as the grains lasted, but later refused the god's love and withered away. In Virgil's *Aeneid*, the Trojan hero Aeneas visits the Sibyl for guidance in reaching the underworld (see also Cleft in the Earth, page 100).

The cave system at Wookey Hole includes what legend says is a witch's cave. In 1912 the ancient body of a woman was found in a shallow grave in 1912 by Herbert Balch, a local archaeologist and geologist who spent years exploring the Mendip Hills; next to her were the remains of two goats, a bowl, a dagger, a latch lifter and an alabaster ball.

Mother Shipton's cave in North Yorkshire is also associated with a particular witch figure, in this case the seer and prophetess. A 1537 letter from Henry VIII to the Duke of Norfolk refers to a "witch of York", although there is no reason to identify this with Mother Shipton, a real figure whose story was enormously elaborated by fraudsters. Nevertheless, we can learn something about witches and witchcraft from the fact that the pool in the cave named after her can apparently turn objects to stone, and Mother Shipton herself has therefore been linked with the story of the Rollright Stones in Oxfordshire (see Standing Stone, page 76).

All these stories connect with two features of the witch: her stonelike and impermeable body, and her mysterious power to create and transform. The witch has a hard, postmenopausal body, but also one that has experienced the radical changes of puberty, pregnancy and menopause. Frightening in its ability to survive change, it also terrifies by its changeability. The darkness of the cave symbolizes the dark unknowability of the body.

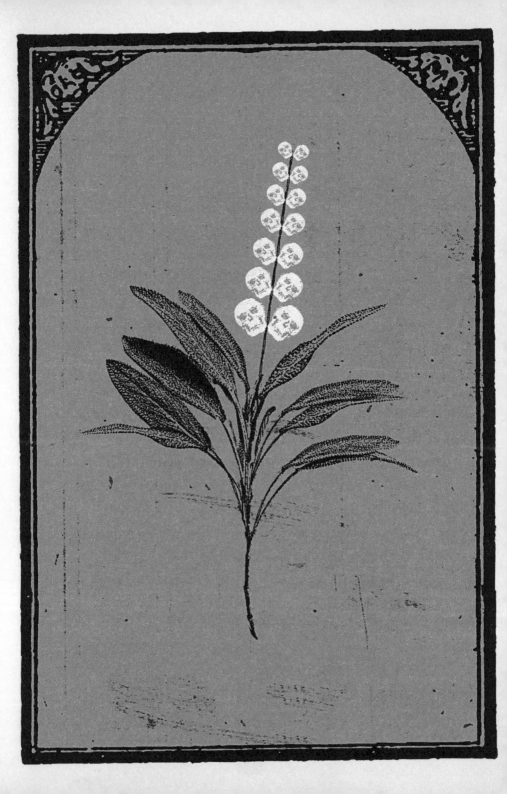

SAGE

Some people say it smells a little like dried blood, which probably explains its many magical uses. If you grow some in your garden, it's said that the woman of the house is dominant. But since sage means wisdom, perhaps this is a kind of compliment. It also has many medicinal properties; the botanical name is *Salvia*, a Latin word with connotations of both *healing* and *health*. *Saga* is just one of the many Latin words for a witch or wise woman.

There is a particular seasonal association between gathering sage for cleansing at Lughnasa or Lammas, August 1; it's a kind of parallel harvest, and it can go with using a stock or sheaf of grain as part of the bundle.

In folklore, sage is associated with love divination. For this, sage must be gathered on Halloween, the eve of All Saints' Day, and the woman must go out into the garden alone at midnight. While the clock strikes 12, she must pluck nine sage leaves, one at every stroke up to the ninth. If she is destined to be married, she will see the face of her husband. If not, she will see a coffin. Sage is also supposed to be plucked on St Mark's Eve, April 25, for the same purpose (see Seasons of the Witch, page 156).

Burning sage has become a fashionable cleansing ritual, often called smudging, but it has no historical basis in Western witchcraft, and runs the risk of being a cultural appropriation. If you do like to use sage, you don't need to order very expensive sage – simply grow your own, as a wise woman can. If you like this ritual, but don't feel comfortable waving a flaming bundle of herbs around your house, a good option is to infuse either oil or water with sage, so that it can be sprayed.

SALT

Arguably the most ancient ritual substance of all. It's a cleansing substance in very many rites; one of the simplest cleansing rituals is to dissolve salt in water, and sprinkle it using a ritual dagger around the area to be cleansed. This can be transformed into a protective ritual where the same salt water is sprinkled on windows and doorways. Everyone would once have been familiar with the use of salt as a preservative for meat and fish, a preventer of decay.

Such cleansing rituals may well have very ancient origins. Like modern Latin Americans, the Romans dedicated a special day to remembering the dead, February 21, and offerings included a few grains of salt. Salt was a gift to the dead, but it was also an effort to keep them in the ground.

As part of magical dealings with the dead – as, indeed, with dealings involving any other summoned power or spirit – control was critical. In an age when corpses were kept in the house for the interval between death and burial, it was common to place a dish of salt on the breast of the corpse as soon as possible after death, and it remained there until the body was placed in the coffin; in the Highlands, the salt was mixed with earth. The preservative qualities of salt made it an ideal symbol of eternity, and it kept away evil spirits – and might have prevented the spirit of the dead person from returning to the body. Another magic involving salt was to sprinkle salt on the floor after a visitor left the house – to prevent their return.

It is always unlucky to spill salt, but the bad luck could be turned aside if the person who spilled the salt picked up a pinch and threw it over his left shoulder. Spilled salt could also be used for divination. The bad luck of the spill landed especially on the person towards whom the salt fell. Another saying connects salt with tears: every grain of spilled salt represents a tear to be cried in future.

CHIMNEY

The chimney is one of the places where the house is open to the world outside. In earlier periods, the chimney had to be charmed against evil intrusions, and most often, old shoes could be bricked up in the chimney to ward off evil (see Witch Marks, page 30). Images survive showing witches coming down the chimney to torment members of a household.

Why is the chimney particularly vulnerable? One reason is the association between fire, soot and magic. Ironically, we still encourage children to believe in a chimney demon, albeit one that has been Christianized. Santa Claus/Father Christmas comes down the chimney, wearing the bright red of a devil. In many countries, he is accompanied by a figure who is covered in soot, called Black Peter in the Netherlands. Recent representations of Peter have been problematically racist and colonial, but originally Peter's colour came from the chimney and the fire that had burned in it.

In the area around Milan, the grimy figure is the witch Befana, who gives children candy shaped like coals. Elsewhere in Europe, the figure is diabolical. Krampus is a horned, anthropomorphic figure in the Central and Eastern Alpine folklore of Europe who, during the Advent season, scares children who have misbehaved. Assisting Saint Nicholas, or Santa Claus, the pair visit children on the night of December 6, with Saint Nicholas rewarding the well-behaved children with gifts such as oranges, dried fruit, walnuts and chocolate, while the badly behaved ones receive only punishment from Krampus with birch rods. This figure is believed to originate from stories of house spirits such as kobolds or elves. The Krampus may also relate to the entourage of an ancient goddess, Frau Perchta, whose frightening masks were displayed in processions on January 6. Perchten are associated with midwinter and the embodiment of fate and the souls of the dead. However, the name also means the brightness of light on snow, and the beauty of age and wisdom.

HEX

A specific word for *curse*, but one with its own special associations. When modern pagans first began to call themselves witches, they were eager to claim that they never hexed anybody; in a strange echo of denials by accused witches during the years of persecution, they claimed that they could do good and would never do harm, because "what you send out, returns to you threefold" – a concept known as the Rule of Three, proposed by Gerald Gardner. This toothless idea of witch power was destined not to survive the presidency of Donald Trump. Many witches – at least partly in jest – decided they had had enough. Since then, Trump has been hexed many times, albeit without noticeable effect.

What kind of curse is this? The short answer is that this depends on the intention. Some witches have explained that the hex is simply a wake-up call. Rather than disorderly, a hex can be a bid to restore order when it has been disrupted. Some witches argued that balance requires them to combine hexing Trump with giving light and energy to, for example, the Georgia Senate Democrats (who duly won). Other punk witches clearly intended harm, and were not deterred by the rule of three. Punk group Dream Nails, who describe themselves as punk witches, used a video to really put the frighteners on the patriarchy with deliberately provocative language, even echoing the traditional African-American hoodoo folkway of hotfoot.

Witches have previous. In the 1960s, W.I.T.C.H. (originally known as Women's International Terrorist Conspiracy from Hell and now the altogether nicer-sounding Women Inspired to Tell their Collective History) organized protests across the country to stand for women's rights. Even before that, the hallmark of the witch during the years of persecution was her power to curse, her verbal fluency in abuse and the theatre of her power (see also Curse, page 148). A woman outspoken enough to speak her rage was seen as a threat to everybody. In the play *The Witch of Edmonton*, Elizabeth Sawyer decides if she has the name, she might just as well have the game too, and voluntarily becomes a witch. It's worth considering.

CIRCLE CASTING

Like a cave, like a house, a circle is an enclosed space, a space that protects. Magic is always a double-edged sword: the more powerful it is, the more the user needs to make sure that she is protected. The circle does not summon and is not itself the magic. Like any other activity, magic requires a safe space and a sense of security, and the circle provides that. It protects, creating an amulet that surrounds the magic user. Many circles historically involve the use of protective names, just as amulets do.

Tradition illustrates this protective function: circle magic may come from efforts to protect women in labour from the demon Lilith, who hungers for their newborn children. A circle can be cast with the athame, the ritual sword (or a favourite kitchen knife). The power of the circle comes partly from its endlessness, so it can be replaced by the pentangle or the endless knot (see Witch Marks, page 30). Opposing powers cannot find a port of entry. The endlessness also refers to the need for perseverance in the ritual. Above all, magic users cannot leave the circle while still performing the magic, and interruptions are regarded as especially dangerous. Indeed, the whole point of circle magic is to create a space away from the infiltration of whatever is dark and terrible, in which further magical endeavours might take place.

However, in the past, Dr Faustus and other black magicians used the circle to protect themselves from the demons they summoned. Such entities mirror the men who summon them in their ambition and ruthlessness. Even theatre audiences found the circular dances of devils on stage terrifying. At a performance of Christopher Marlowe's play *Doctor Faustus* in Exeter, the actors themselves became convinced that there was "one devil too many among them", and fled the stage in a panic. The message of the circle is to be careful who you call.

PENDANT

There are plenty of people who want to sell you pendants with witchcraft symbols on them, and if you find them pretty and empowering, or scary in a good way, there's absolutely no harm in them. However, the only magic they possess is a mix of your ideas about them and their cultural meaning. Elsewhere in this book (see, for example, Witch Marks, pages 30 and 32), protective markings are described, and the particular power of an endless shape like the circle or pentacle, a shape without openings. The pentacle is abundantly present in pendants marketed as witch-related, and every necklace mimics the circle. Modern witchcraft doesn't pay enough attention to protective magic in general, in part because it is overly keen to be pretty. A pretty girl on a broomstick isn't going to scare anybody.

Alternatively, and perhaps more traditionally, a pendant might be associated with a wish to attract rather than repel. Many of these take the form of knots, in accurate imitation of binding spells. Others take the form of small bottles, although these do not imitate the witch bottle, or Bellarmine, of the past, but instead imitate a potion. Since much of magic is about imitation and sympathy, such creations could be seen as positive and intelligent redeployments of older ideas for a modern world.

Pendants can also be seen as connected to binding spells, including the recent development of a lock magic ritual. A love lock or love padlock is a padlock that couples lock to a bridge, fence, gate, monument or similar public fixture to symbolize their love. Names or initials, and perhaps the date, are inscribed on the padlock, and its key is thrown away (often into a nearby river) to symbolize unbreakable love. Since the 2000s, love locks have proliferated at an increasing number of locations worldwide. A pendant attached not to a person but to an architectural site is a recent incarnation of ancient ideas.

DIANA

In the diocese of Burchard of Worms, during the 11th century, the women believed in *silvaticae*, "wild women" of the woods who "showed themselves at will to their lovers and when they had taken their pleasure with them, hid or vanished at their will". We know about them because Burchard was putting together some notes for priests hearing confession. Another clergyman, Martin of Braga, says evil spirits of the wood call themselves Dianas, while the monk Regino of Prüm wrote in the tenth century:

> Certain criminal women, who have turned back to Satan and are seduced by illusions of his demons and phantasms, believe and avow openly that during the night hours they ride on certain beasts together with Diana, the goddess of the pagans, and an uncounted host of women that pass over many lands in the silence of the dead of night; that they obey her orders as those of a mistress; and that on certain nights they are summoned to her service.

This Diana is like, but not the same as, the classical deity of the ancient Romans. She was goddess of the Moon and also goddess of hunting and wild animals. She probably at least partly derived from the Greek goddess Artemis, and was particularly the goddess not only of wild nature, but also of both menstruation and childbirth. The medieval goddess, however, has become a goddess of witches and is connected with fairies: the Rumanian word for *fairy* is derived from her name.

In these figures, which are connected by other Catholic clergy with other pagan goddesses such as the German Frau Holda, we can see the emerging idea of witches gathering together to fly by night into the dark and the wild (see Flight, page 50). Some scholars have connected this idea with reports of night battles in the skies between witches and other powerful magic users to ensure the fertility of the land and of flocks. It is because of Diana that some modern pagans consider themselves to be Dianic witches, grounding their magical practices in goddess worship.

BROOMSTICK

Brooms and witches have been with us for ever. A broom consists of stiff, thin lengths or twigs, tied to a longer and thicker staff. It was used to push substances around and out of the house, and it symbolized not only cleansing but the maintenance of the borders of the domestic. A broom brings together a carefully shaped, man-made staff with the wildness of twigs, and deploys both to make dust fly.

The iconic broomstick is part of the feminization of the figure of the witch, and yet the first witch recorded riding a broomstick was male, Guillaume Edelin, an Augustinian prior in the town of Saint-Germain-en-Laye. He had preached that witchcraft and sorcery were not real, but only peasant superstitions. Convicted in 1453, he spent the rest of his life in prison. His case shows the way ideas about witchcraft can gather momentum quickly. What probably cements the place of the broom in witchcraft is the Lancashire witch trial of 1612, where a woodcut in the pamphlet shows a woman on a broomstick, and Reginald Scot, author of *The Discoverie of Witchcraft*, who says that all the witches who dance at the Sabbath have brooms in their hands

Brooms are fraught with magic. Some of the magic might come from the plant called broom. English folklore tells us that if you sweep the house with broom in May you will sweep the head of the house away. Sweeping dust out of the house is ill-advised, because it means sweeping luck away. Lay a broom across the doorstep to protect the house from strangers; stand it up in the corner, and strangers will come in. Laying a broom across a doorway is also a way of identifying a witch – when the witch comes past, she would be obliged to pick it up. The broom can be sexual too: if a girl steps over a broom handle she will be a mother before she is a wife, and if an unmarried woman has child, she has jumped the broom.

INDEX

Images are indicated by *italics*.

FURTHER READING

Afterlives: Return of the Dead in the Middle Ages, Nancy Mandeville Caciola (2016)

Albion: Guide to Legendary Britain, Jennifer Beatrice Westwood (1985)

Ancient Astrology, Tamysn Barton (1994)

Archaeology of Ritual and Magic, Ralph Merrifield (1987)

Aspects of Anglo-Saxon Magic, Bill Griffiths (2022)

Astrology, Psychology, and the Four Elements: An Energy Approach to Astrology and its Use in the Counseling Arts, Stephen Arroyo (1978)

At the Bottom of the Garden: Dark History of Fairies, Hobgoblins, Nymphs, and Other Troublesome Things, Diane Purkiss (2001)

Befana is Returning: The Story of a Tuscan Festival, Steve Siporin (2022)

Behind the Crystal Ball: Magic and Science from Antiquity to the New Age, Anthony F. Aveni (1996)

Bohemian Gothic Tarot, Karen Mahony and Alex Ukolov (2007)

Buried Soul: How Humans Invented Death, Timothy Taylor (2004)

Queen of Wands: Story of Pamela Colman Smith, the Artist Behind the Rider-Waite Tarot Deck, Cat Willet (2022)

Celtic Myths That Shape the Way We Think, M.A. Williams (2021)

Charms, Charmers and Charming: International Research on Verbal Magic, Jonathan Roper (2008)

Children of Ash and Elm: History of the Vikings, Neil S. Price (2020)

Crossroads of Conjure: Roots and Practices of Granny Magic, Hoodoo, Brujeria, and Curanderismo, Katrina Rasbold (2019)

Cunning-Folk and Familiar Spirits: Shamanistic Visionary Traditions in Early Modern British Witchcraft and Magic, Emma Wilby (2005)

Dictionary of British Folk-Tales in the English Language, Katharine Briggs (1991)

Dictionary of Celtic Myth and Legend, Miranda J. Green (1992)

Dictionary of Celtic Mythology (Oxford Reference Collection), James MacKillop (2016)

Dictionary of English Folklore, Jacqueline Simpson and Steve Roud (2016)

Dictionary of Fairies: Hobgoblins, Brownies, Bogies and Other Supernatural Creatures, Katharine M. Briggs (1976)

Dictionary of Plant-Lore, Roy Vickery (1997)

Dictionary of Superstitions, Iona Opie (2009)

Discerning Spirits: Divine and Demonic Possession in the Middle Ages, Nancy Mandeville Caciola (2003)

Drawing Down the Moon: Magic in the Ancient Greco-Roman World, Radcliffe G. Edmonds III. (2019)

Element Encyclopedia of Witchcraft: Complete A–Z for the Entire Magical World, Judika Illes (2005)

English Year, Steve Roud (2008)

Fabled Coast: Legends & Traditions from Around the Shores of Britain & Ireland, Sophia Kingshill and Jennifer Beatrice Westwood (2014)

Fated Sky: Astrology in History, Benson Bobrick (2006)

Greek and Roman Necromancy, Daniel Ogden (2019)

Greek Magical Papyri in Translation, Including the Demotic Spells: Texts v. 1, Hans Dieter Betz (1997)

Grimoires: History of Magic Books, Owen Davies (2010)

Gypsies: An English History, David Cressy (2018)

Hekate Soteira: Study of Hekate's Roles in the Chaldean Oracles and Related Literature (Homage Series): 21 (Society for Classical Studies American Classical Studies), Sarah Iles Johnston (1990)

Hellenistic Astrology: Study of Fate and Fortune, Chris Brennan (2017)

History of Magic, Witchcraft and the Occult, Suzannah Lipscombe (2020)

History of Western Astrology Volume I: The Ancient World, Nicholas Campion (2009)

History of Western Astrology Volume II: Medieval and Modern Worlds, Nicholas Campion (2009)

Last Witch Craze: John Aubrey, the Royal Society and the Witches, Tony McAleavy (2022)

Leaping Hare, George Ewart Evans and David Thomson (2017)

Leechcraft: Early English Charms, Plantlore, and Healing,
Stephen Pollington (2022)

*Little Book of Witchcraft: Beginner's Guide to White Witchcraft
and Spells for Every Occasion,* Astrid Carvel (2017)

Lore of Scotland: Guide to Scottish Legends, Jennifer Westwood
and Sophia Kingshill (2012)

*Lore of the Land: Guide to England's Legends, from Spring-
heeled Jack to the Witches of Warboys,* Jacqueline Simpson
and Jennifer Westwood (2005)

Lost Gods of England, Brian Branston (1974)

*Magic and Witchery in the Modern West: Celebrating the
Twentieth Anniversary of 'Triumph of the Moon',* Shai Feraro
and Ethan Doyle White (2019)

Magic in Merlin's Realm: History of Occult Politics in Britain,
Francis Young (2022)

*Magical Britain: 650 Enchanted and Mystical Sites – From
Healing Wells and Secret Shrines to Giants' Strongholds and
Fairy Glens,* Rob Wildwood (2022)

Milk: An Intimate History of Breastfeeding, Joanna Wolfarth
(2023)

New Forest Myths and Folklore, Brice Stratford (2022)

Njal's Saga, translated by Leifur Eiricksson (2002)

Norse Mythology for Smart People
norse-mythology.org/

Norse Myths That Shape the Way We Think, Carolyne
Larrington (2023)

*Pagan Religions of the Ancient British Isles: Their Nature and
Legacy,* Ronald Hutton (1991)

Pagans: Visual Culture of Pagan Myths, Legends and Rituals,
Ethan Doyle White (2023)

Parkers' Astrology, Derek and Julia Parker (1991)

*Peace-Weavers and Shield-Maidens: Women in Early English
Society,* Kathleen Herbert (2022)

Penguin Guide to the Superstitions of Britain and Ireland, Steve
Roud (2006)

*Perceptions of the Prehistoric in Anglo-Saxon England: Religion,
Ritual, and Rulership in the Landscape* (*Medieval History and
Archaeology*), Sarah Semple (2019)

Physical Evidence for Ritual Acts, Sorcery and Witchcraft in Christian Britain: Feeling for Magic, Ronald Hutton (Ed.) (2015)

Plant Magick. Library of Esoterica, Jessica Hundley (2022)

Poetic Edda, Carolyne Larrington (2014)

Popular Magic: Cunning-Folk in English History, Owen Davies (2007) *Prehistory of Sex: Four Million Years of Human Sexual Culture*, Timothy L. L. Taylor (1997)

Queens of the Wild: Pagan Goddesses in Christian Europe: An Investigation, Ronald Hutton (2022)

Reformation of the Landscape: Religion, Identity, and Memory in Early Modern Britain and Ireland, Alexandra Walsham (2012)

Restless Dead: Encounters Between the Living and the Dead in Ancient Greece, Sarah Iles Johnston (1999).

Sarn Helen: A Journey Through Wales, Past, Present and Future, Tom Bullough and Jackie Morris (2023)

Scheme of Heaven: Astrology and the Birth of Science, Alexander Boxer (2020)

Science of the Magical: From the Holy Grail to Love Potions to Superpowers, Matt Kaplan (2015)

Seer in Ancient Greece, Michael Flower (2009)

Stopping Places: A Journey Through Gypsy Britain, Damian Le Bas (2019)

Tarot: History, Mystery and Lore, Cynthia Giles (1994)

Trees in Anglo-Saxon England: Literature, Lore and Landscape, Della Hooke (2013)

Triumph of the Moon: A History of Modern Pagan Witchcraft, Ronald Hutton (1999)

Twelve Faces of the Goddess: Transform Your Life with Astrology, Magick, and the Sacred Feminine, Danielle Blackwood (2018)

Twilight of the Godlings: Shadowy Beginnings of Britain's Supernatural Beings, Francis Young (2023)

Two Madonnas: Politics of Festival in a Sardinian Community, Sabina Magliocco (2006)

Understanding Aleister Crowley's Thoth Tarot: New Edition, Lon Milo DuQuette (2017)

Victorian Romantic Tarot Deck: Based on Original Victorian Engravings, Karen Mahony and Alex Ukolov (2006)

Viking Way: Magic and Mind in Late Iron Age Scandinavia, 2nd Edition, Neil Price (2019)

Visions of Isobel Gowdie: Magic, Shamanism and Witchcraft in Seventeenth-Century Scotland, Emma Wilby (2010)

We Borrow the Earth: An Intimate Portrait of the Gypsy Folk Tradition and Culture, Patrick Jasper Lee (2015)

Wild Once: Awaken the Magic Within. Unleash True Power, Vivianne Crowley (2022)

Winter Goddess: Percht, Holda, and Related Figures, Folklore, Vol. 95, No. 2, pp.151–166, Lotte Motz (1984)

Witch in History: Early Modern and Twentieth-Century Representations, Diane Purkiss (1996)

Witch: History of Fear, From Ancient Times to the Present, Ronald Hutton (2017)

Witchcraft and Magic in Europe: Ancient Greece and Rome, Bengt Ankarloo and Stuart Clark (1999)

Witchcraft and Secret Societies of Rural England: Magic of Toadmen, Plough Witches, Mummers, and Bonesmen, Nigel Pennick (2019)

Witchcraft. The Library of Esoterica, Jessica Hundley (Ed.) and Pam Grossman (Co Ed.) (2021)

Witchcraft: History in Thirteen Trials, Marion Gibson (2023)

Witches of St Osyth: Persecution, Betrayal and Murder in Elizabethan England, Marion Gibson (2022)

Witching Culture Folklore and Neo-Paganism in America, Sabina Magliocco (2010)

Women of the Golden Dawn: Rebels and Priestesses – Maud Gonne, Moina Bergson Mathers, Annie Horniman, Florence Farr, Mary Greer (1996)

First published in 2024 by Welbeck
An Imprint of HEADLINE PUBLISHING GROUP

1

Cataloguing in Publication Data is available from the British Library

ISBN 9781802797220

Printed and bound in Dubai

Headline's policy is to use papers that are natural, renewable and recyclable
products and made from wood grown in well-managed forests and other
controlled sources. The logging and manufacturing processes are expected
to conform to the environmental regulations of the country of origin.

HEADLINE PUBLISHING GROUP
An Hachette UK Company
Carmelite House
50 Victoria Embankment
London EC4Y 0DZ

www.headline.co.uk
www.hachette.co.uk